Public Policy
on the Status
of Women

Public Policy on the Status of Women

Agenda and Strategy for the 70s

Irene L. Murphy

Lexington Books
D.C. Heath and Company
Lexington, Massachusetts
Toronto   London

Library of Congress Cataloging in Publication Data

Murphy, Irene Lyons.
    Public policy on the status of women.
      1. Woman—Rights of women.   2. Women in
the United States.   I. Title.
HQ1426.M9   323.1   73-9658
ISBN 0-669-90316-7

Second printing December 1974.

Published simultaneously in Canada.

Printed in the United States of America.

International Standard Book Number: 0-669-90316-7

Library of Congress Catalog Card Number: 73-9658

To my mother, Marie A. Lyons, who, in her own way, has been a staunch feminist all of her life

Contents

Foreword

American feminists, now embarking on the second half of the second century of struggle for equality, who look for a swift and sure way to achieve their goals, will do well to read this book with care. Its objective, analytical approach to feminism as a political issue offers appropriate guidelines for the movement to follow. As advocates for equal rights for women pinpoint goals, they need to understand more fully the devious paths public policy sometimes takes, and to maximize their potentially powerful and plentiful resources for change. The means at hand are described in this sound and well-documented volume that is a unique and major contribution to the annals of the women's movement.

A prodigious amount of research lends belief to the basic hypothesis that women can utilize public policy to achieve equality in the 1970s. Agreement on goals is widespread (despite the well-publicized efforts of a few conservative women, abetted by some labor leaders, to sidetrack ratification of the Equal Rights Amendment). A wide range of well-established women's groups whose past interest in feminism has been slight or nonexistent, is increasingly working for the rights of women. Strong and knowledgeable support from blue-collar and other working-class women is growing as understanding of the true universality of the feminist movement spreads.

Irene Murphy clarifies, by combing through an array of federal programs and their functions, the exact form a major lobbying effort should take. Heretofore, answers to questions about federal policy on the status of women have been scattered piecemeal in a variety of pamphlets and newsletters, many of them worthy contributions to an understanding of the movement, but often not readily available. All who have attempted to follow the course of federal policy—and from time to time to influence it—will be grateful for the one-volume reference file contained herein.

Careful attention is paid to the failures and inconsistencies of present public policy on the status of women, beginning with the lack of support provided by the Nixon Administration. As in other issue areas, Congress has been pressured to add strength and meaning to federal policy. Dr. Murphy traces the work of what she rightly calls "the watershed 92nd Congress" as it dealt with a myriad of bills affecting economic and educational opportunities for women. Its accomplishments described, the steps still to be taken are set forth in a detailed agenda—an appropriate laundry list for feminists in the seventies. Beside a set of achievable goals, positive and practical techniques are suggested so that a true improvement in the status of women may be registered for recording by the 1980 census.

Women's groups fighting for equality for the most part now represent professional and executive women, and housewives with college and graduate degrees. Their participation is indispensable, and now the movement is reaching out to the leadership and support of representatives of the vast majority of women who are just beginning to become involved, minorities, working-class women, women returning to work without skills or in other ways confronted with the problems that unequal status has foisted upon them.

I recommend this book for the depth of its analysis of the political side of the feminist issue. It is a gold mine of data about public policy, a proper introduction to the subject which suggests a number of related issues for further specialized study. It offers factual evidence that the achievement of equality for women and the realization of their full contribution to their nation can be resolved before the end of this decade.

Bernice Sandler
Director, Project on the
Status and Education of Women,
Association of American Colleges.

Acknowledgments

Research for this study was conducted under a grant from the Eagleton Institute of Politics, Policy Research Associates Program. I want to thank Don Herzberg, former Director of Eagleton, and Alan Rosenthal, its Associate Director, for the opportunity thus offered to finish this study. The atmosphere at Eagleton is conducive to friendly discussions and sharpened insights, and was of benefit to me. Ruth Mandel and Ida Schmertz of the Center for the American Woman and Politics at Eagleton offered firm and beneficial guidance at strategic phases of research and writing. Under their leadership the Center will do well.

I have had immense help from several sources. Bert Hartry and Clare Kabel did excellent research on federal programs and their legislative histories. Catherine East, Dr. Bernice Sandler, and Morag Simchak command an extensive knowledge of the subject matter of this book. Their presence in the movement has had an immeasurably great impact on it. I have benefited from their writings, their speeches, and conversations with them.

Countless participants in, and experts about, the political side of feminism have contributed to the completion of this study. Members of federal program and congressional committee staffs have responded to requests for data readily and accurately; so have many women associated with feminist groups—particularly Arvonne Fraser of WEAL, Ann Scott of NOW, and Doris Meissner and Jane MacMichael of NWPC. Marguerite Rawalt, who has amiably and accurately provided many a ready answer to questions on legal discrimination against women, deserves a special vote of thanks. I am indebted to Elizabeth Koenig Van Bergen for help with the survey of women's organizations.

The Kennedy Commission on the Status of Women, and the 1970 Task Force on Women's Rights and Responsibilities, reviewed national policy on the status of women and set goals for it. The work of the many women involved in both contributed substantially to this study.

Irene L. Murphy

Introduction

This book is for all those who want to know more about the formation of national policy on equality for women and the factors most likely to influence its future course. It is hoped that it will provoke discussion and stimulate research of an analytical nature into the politics of the women's movement. Those who want equal status for women need to probe past policy decisions for a thorough understanding of their development, if they want to play a conclusive role in their future control.

Most of the literature of today's women's rights movement is written to convince the reader of the justice of feminist goals, or to tell how women feel or should feel about them. If it deals at all with national policy on the status of women, it is concerned with the frequency or extent of discrimination. It has not yet come to grips with feminism as a national political issue. A review of the activities of the new groups which have sprung up to change the life-style of women shows almost all of them to be deeply political, to care about the formation of policy and to want to influence it. The "women's rights lobby," a loosely structured network of organizations based on or near Capitol Hill, with a supporting network of thousands of local affiliates, has produced its own "literature" about legislative and administrative decisions affecting sex discrimination. Handouts, newsletters and reports have proliferated over the years, serving the immediate purpose of alerting members to the need for lobbying on the Hill, or in their home territories.

Overall studies of the formation of national policy on the status of women, using the analytical methods of political science, have not been attempted. This study should be considered an introductory effort to fill that gap. Each sub-issue under the broad umbrella of women's rights deserves its own separate study, in terms of the commitment to the national goals it embraces, the nature of group- and constituent- demand for it, and the response it has brought from national decision-makers.

The present assignment, by the very nature of the topic and the dearth of analytical studies about it, has been a difficult one. To avoid superficiality on the one hand, and overwhelming volume on the other, posed problems of organization and data selection which were not easily resolved. In an effort to provide boundaries for the subject matter, national policy on the status of women has been defined as involving decisions directly related to sex discrimination, as it applies to legal and economic status. National policy in this issue area has been affected peripherally by many other policy decisions, and by the decisions of state courts and legislatures as well. Action taken by the Congress and the president about matters closely affecting women's legal and economic rights has been considered a proper subject for this study. Topics that deserve separate, in-depth analyses would include abortion reform, the participation by women in political party policy-making, their voting behavior, and other related areas.

1

National policy on the status of women has been treated in this analysis like any public policy issue area. Before it became part of national policy, goals had to be described and commitments made. What were these, as they touched on equality for women? As demand grew for the commitment of federal resources to achieve goals, how was it expressed, and how did the president and Congress respond? What kind of programs were established? Do they satisfy demand for output or are they under stress and asked to do more than they are able, in terms of resources assigned to them? What kind of constituency supports or opposes demand for greater output? And what compromises have resulted? This study will attempt to provide some of the answers to these questions as it describes the way in which the president and Congress have responded in recent years to requests for action by a resurgent feminist movement.

The development of feminism in the United States, since its beginning in the early part of the nineteenth century, has received increasing attention from historians. Although the past always has bearing on present policy, this study will refer to the past experience of feminism only occasionally, concentrating rather on policy as it existed at the end of the Johnson presidency, and as it reacted to the burgeoning women's movement of the late sixties and early seventies. It will begin with a review of the commitment to equality for women* United States leaders have repeated over a long period of time. And it will describe the more specific goals which have become a part of a grand consensus, supported by a wide variety of women's groups.

National decision-makers made only one limited commitment—the Women's Bureau—to public policy on the status of women, after granting suffrage, until the sixties, when sex discrimination was added to a string of policy decisions providing for equality for minorities. Important developments in national policy on the status of women did not take place until the beginning of the first Nixon administration. Nixon was, thus, the first president since Woodrow Wilson to experience the pressures of a strongly political feminist movement.

The major portion of this analysis will deal with White House and congressional response to demand for strong national commitments to end sex discrimination that was both legal and economic. The almost total lack of support for positive national policy in these areas on the part of the President and his administration (Chapter 2) has resulted in greater pressure on Congress to bolster women's rights programs. These programs, designed to end discrimination in private and public employment, failed to satisfy women. Women's groups turned to Congress during the first Nixon administration to add strength and leadership to them (Chapter 3).

The continued gap between the rhetoric of national commitment and the reality of woman's status brought new converts to the feminist movement from the late sixties on. Despite its growth in numbers, it has been accused of harboring an elitist leadership. The facts behind the assumption need to

---

* Women are, of course, both white and black and represent all of the minorities men do, despite the disconcerting habit of policy makers to refer continually to "women *and* minorities."

be examined, along with the attitudes of working women toward equal rights groups (Chapter 4). The latter have developed an agenda for national policy with which few women's organizations disagree. Knowledge about the detailed goals of optimal national policy is prerequisite to its achievement. Specific goals are outlined in some detail in Chapter 5. Women presently lack power as policy makers in government and in political parties. What strategies will maximize their resources as they attempt to move Congress and the president to meet the goals of full equality? What allies do they need and what compromises might they have to make to achieve their goals and to improve the status of women to the extent that, for the first time in decades, improvement will be reflected in the census of 1980? The last chapter describes strategy and tactics which will be needed for the achievement of optimal national policy on the status of women.

As a policy analysis of an important issue area, this study is designed to advance knowledge about the national decision-making process; as an application of the tools developed by political science, it focusses on the major factors involved in an issue area which has been blurred in the course of national debate although, perhaps, no more than any other.

Feminism is a political movement to the extent to which it mobilizes efforts to alter public policy. It needs to be better understood, as part of our national commitment to the ideals and goals of democracy.

1 The Gap Between Rhetoric and Reality

In the late 1960s and early 1970s feminists were fond of quoting the "declaration of independence" their movement-founders had fashioned at the first recorded meeting which dealt exclusively with women's rights—the famous gathering at Seneca Falls, New York, in 1848. They seemed to like its uppity tone, its succinct analyses:

The history of mankind is a history of repeated injuries and usurpations on the part of man toward woman, having in direct object the establishment of an absolute tyranny over her.[1]

The early collaboration of Lucretia Mott and Elizabeth Cady Stanton pinpointed national goals for the status of women for generations to come. The truth was held "to be self-evident that all men *and women* [author's emphasis, but unquestionably their's, too] are created equal" and there was no escaping the fact that American ideals, both legal and economic, were intended for women as well as men. Full equality would abolish two kinds of discrimination. First, the Declaration and its Resolutions called for an end to all laws that conflicted in any way "with the true and substantial happiness of woman." Second, the authors asked for equal pay and employment opportunity when they resolved

that the speedy success of our cause depends upon the zealous and untiring efforts of both men and women, for the overthrow of the monopoly of the pulpit, and for the securing to woman an equal participation with men in the various trades, professions, and commerce.[2]

American policy makers have had greater problems with the realities of the Seneca Falls Declaration than they have had with its rhetoric. Ironically, several of the participants in the meeting believed that it was going too far to ask for the vote. In more than a hundred years of piecemeal feminist efforts, woman suffrage was the only national policy goal achieved. In 1961, just as if the Declaration had been inscribed the day before, President John F. Kennedy felt it necessary to call for a national commission to recommend guidelines for national policy on the status of women. His rhetoric sounded a familiar theme "Full realization of women's basic rights," he declared to be "part of our Nation's commitment to human dignity, freedom and democracy."[3] The first presidential advisory body to undertake a review of the subject, under the leadership of Eleanor Roosevelt, was charged with seeking ways to remove the barriers to sexual equality, discriminatory legislation, and lack of economic opportunity. But in 1970, the Task Force on Women's Rights and Responsibilities, appointed by President Richard M.

5

Nixon, again warned that "the quality of life to which we aspire and the questioning at home and abroad of our commitment to the democratic ideal, make it imperative that our nation utilize to the fullest the potential of all citizens."[4] Ideals remained the same, but little had been accomplished toward their achievement.

National Goals Elaborated

During the sixties the more detailed needs for improved national policy on the status of women began to emerge from the collective discussions of official advisory bodies such as the Kennedy commission, the first of the more militant feminist groups like the National Organization for Women, and a few researchers[5] who had begun to take an interest in the failures of official policies to end sex discrimination. Once again, there was agreement not only on major purposes, but on many of the more detailed agenda items that groups and individuals began to circulate. This agreement crossed party lines, income levels, religious persuasions, types of occupation and educational status. The 1963 report of the Kennedy commission had opted for a long series of goals, including child care services, equality of social security benefits, appointment of women to high level government positions, and an executive order which would extend fair employment contract compliance to women. By 1969, the Nixon Task Force had moved to the left of its Democratic counterpart; it had endorsed the Equal Rights Amendment, endorsed enforcement power to the Equal Employment Opportunity Commission, and had suggested that the President appoint an assistant in the White House to be in charge of an Office of Women's Rights and Responsibilities,—that assistant to report directly to the president.

Party platforms became similarly explicit in 1972. The Republicans listed no fewer than nine specific items, including not only ratification of the Amendment, but also elimination of discrimination in credit, in the criminal justice system, and at all levels of the federal government. The Democrats had already gone on record in favor of all of these, plus the granting of cease and desist power to the Equal Opportunity Commission for stricter enforcement of the federal law against sex discrimination, extension of equal pay to all workers, including domestic workers, and other detailed items.

By the early seventies it was possible to say that a wide range of organizations, which were either feminist in orientation or designed to advance the interest of women in a number of activities, had achieved a consensus on national policy toward the status of women. With occasional exceptions, religious groups, social welfare groups, occupational and professional associations, caucuses within professional and other groups agreed that:

the Equal Rights Amendment should be passed, and subsequently implemented by Congress and state legislatures;

there should be equality in law and practice, with or without the ERA in granting of credit, and in marriage, property, and criminal law;

laws on the books guaranteeing equal opportunity in education, employment, and pay should be enforced, and strengthened where needed.

Despite the consensus which existed among a large number of organizations, and the fact that both parties had endorsed major women's rights goals, there was strong evidence at the beginning of the second Nixon administration, as, indeed, there had been at the start of the first, that by all available measuring standards, the status of women had not only failed to improve for several decades, but had, particularly in economic achievement, actually declined. As results of analyses of the 1970 census became available in 1971 and 1972, it was apparent that there had been a further decline in some areas and no improvement in others. And, as researchers began to explore the question of legal equality in states which had passed their own Equal Rights Amendments, or in anticipation of ratification of the national amendment, discriminatory laws in criminal sentencing, treatment of prostitutes and rape victims, and dozens of other judicial areas were discovered. Research frequently was hampered by failure of state legislatures to support these endeavors, and an apparent reluctance on the part of foundations and government agencies alike to fund projects which appeared to have "uncertain" value to conservative grant-proposal evaluators. In any case, all the available data indicated that the gap between the theory and reality of women's status, before the law and in the job market, was wide; almost as wide as it had been in every decade since "the great leap forward"—the passage of the suffrage amendment in 1920.

Economic Equality

Economically, with respect to their hours and their wages, women are not a sex at all but an underbidding element in a competitive labor market.

> League of Women Voters pamphlet, "Toward
> Equal Rights for Men and Women," 1929.[6]

Federal government statistics, the results of surveys by the Bureau of the Census, the Department of Labor's Bureau of Labor Statistics, and other agencies, contribute to a wealth of data which supports the conclusion that women are segregated into lower paying jobs in both public and private employment. Even when engaged in work equal to or comparable with that performed by men, they are paid less, sometimes by 15 or 20 percent and, most often, by as much as 40 percent or more. Most federal women employees, almost 80 percent, cluster in the bottom six pay grades. Only a few women have been admitted to the armed services, which have employed as much as 4 percent of the total work force, and have been deprived not only of the opportunity to serve their country, but also benefits in education and employment. Furthermore, women cannot even start their own businesses as easily as men, because it is more difficult for them to obtain credit.

8

All these phenomena had continued in the 1960s, despite the passage of legislation in 1963 which guaranteed equal pay for a substantial number of working women, and in 1964 which ended discrimination in employment practices in much of private industry.[7] A contributing factor to the continued low income level of women (minority women are consistently on the very bottom of the ladder—somewhat below white women) is lack of educational opportunity, not only for higher education and professional training, but for vocational training for craft jobs. The failure of women to receive as much education as men has shut them off from advancement in most job and professional categories. When one looks for an explanation for the lack of women in political life, for example, part of that explanation is found in the number of women attorneys (still somewhat less than 5 percent), itself the result of systematic exclusion of women from law schools by the use of strict quota systems. Three bench marks measure the economic status of women: occupation, pay and employment status (i.e., whether they are employed at all), and education.

Occupational Status

The author of a 1969 article entitled "The Declining Status of Women," reached the conclusion that over recent decades "There [had] been a slight but persistent decline in the proportions of professional, technical and kindred workers that were female, while either a definite increase or a leveling occurred for every other category."[8] When 1970 figures became available, it was obvious that no substantial change had taken place. More women worked in lower paying service, blue-collar, and clerical jobs, and fewer in higher paying professional and managerial occupations in 1970 than had in 1950 or 1960. While women maintained their participation in lower paying jobs at an 80 percent level, men were bringing theirs down from about 52 percent in 1950 to 48 percent in 1971. Women participated in professional and technical jobs, and were managers, craftsmen, foremen and farm managers at a rate of 18.9 percent of their total participation in the labor force in 1950, and about 21 percent in 1971. Men, on the other hand, had occupied these higher paid positions at a rate of 47 percent of their total in 1950 and 51.3 percent in 1971.[9]

Figures which show a participation rate of women in professional positions of almost 40 percent of the total employed are misleading. A breakdown of these categories shows that, by far, the largest number of women in this category are in the lower paying professional jobs: teachers, nurses, librarians and social workers. They represent only a small fraction of well-paid professionals, lawyers, doctors, natural scientists, top-ranking professional faculty members, and engineers. The conclusions of the author of the 1969 article are still valid:

First, while there has been an increase in the number of women employed in professions, the percentage increase is considerably less than that of men, and the female has neither displaced nor seriously challenged the American male's dominance in professional positions. Second, greatest relative female increases occurred primarily in those specific categories which already had an overwhelming majority of men—auditors and accountants, personnel and labor-relations workers, sports instructors and officials, physicians and surgeons, lawyers and judges, and public relations workers and publicity writers. Third, in the remaining categories of relatively greater female increase are those occupations uniquely compatible with homemaking responsibilities and thus lend themselves to part-time or irregular patterns of work involvement. [10]

Pay and Unemployment

Women employed in jobs similar to those held by men—waitresses, bank tellers, cleaning women, for example—have frequently been paid less for comparable work. Jobs held predominantly by women, such as executive secretarial positions requiring a high order of skill, pay less than comparable white collar jobs held by men, which automatically fall into managerial categories. Women managers in traditionally female departments (such as bakery departments in supermarkets) are consistently paid less than male managers. Economist Juanita Kreps has explored other aspects of the problem:

Many of the occupational groups in which women are heavily concentrated pay low wages while requiring higher-than-average educational achievement. . . . The median number of years of school completed by males and females in these occupations is higher than the median for the total male labor force; yet the median income (for males or females) in these female dominated occupations does not compare favorably with the median for all male workers. [11]

Pay for women at universities is consistently lower for women faculty members than for men, as numerous studies have affirmed. A 1972 study by the National Education Association saw no change in trends:

The highest proportions of faculty who are women occur in groupings of institutions and classifications of faculty in which salaries of all faculty are lowest. . . . Information from earlier studies in this series shows that during the past 12 years in the institutions reporting salaries by sex, the overall proportion of faculty who are women has increased by 10 percentage points at the instructor rank while it has decreased at each of the higher ranks over this period . . . [12]

While lack of improvement in pay for many occupations was explained by failures of federal programs to push for change in employment opportunity in the federal government itself, and in private industry, there was some promise that extension of the Equal Pay Act to professional, administrative, and executive personnel, might some day be reflected in higher pay for women in all of these categories.

Women employed by the federal government looked for increased activity, too, after 1972 legislation. An "upward mobility" program in effect during the 1968-1972 years had achieved few results. Figures on the employment of women by the federal government bear a close resemblance to those for the economy as a whole. In 1971, 18.5 percent of all the women employed in the federal government were in administrative positions (level 5 and above), requiring college degrees. The other 81.5 percent were in positions calling for minimal or moderate education and experience.[13]

Economic status is quite obviously not only affected by the type of job one has, but also by whether or not one has a job at all. The 1969 Handbook of the Women's Bureau pointed to the fact that women have consistently been without jobs more frequently and for longer periods than men.

The unemployment rate has been higher for women than for men in recent years, and the gap between the two rates has been widening. Following the recession of 1960-61, and the high unemployment rates prevailing in 1961 (7.2 percent for women and 6.4 percent for men), the rates for both women and men declined, but the employment situation did not improve for women as much as it did for men. Women's unemployment remained fairly high at 4.8 percent for 1968, while the rate for men dropped to 2.9 percent.[14]

The highest unemployment rates have been for nonwhite women, with those at the 16- to 20-year-old level substantially higher than for older women, or men. Unemployment for teen-aged nonwhite women is not only higher, but, typically, of longer duration. Unemployment percentages for 1970-71 were as follows:

Rate of Unemployment by Age, Race and Sex, 1970, 1971[15]

Race and Age	Women		Men	
	1971	1970	1971	1970
Minority				
Total 16 years and over	10.8	9.3	9.1	7.3
16-to-19 years	35.5	34.4	28.9	24.9
20 years and over	8.7	6.9	7.2	5.6
White				
Total 16 years and over	6.3	5.4	4.9	4.0
16-to-19 years	15.2	13.3	15.1	13.7
20 years and over	5.3	4.4	4.0	3.2

Lack of child-care facilities has been described as a leading, if not *the* leading factor in unemployment of women in the younger age categories. Three out of five welfare mothers in the late sixties had one or more children under the age of six, and another 30 percent had children between the ages of six and thirteen. Only 10 percent did not need child-care facilities in order to work. Economist Sar Levitan believed that more than child-care services were needed for unemployed women:

Those who have worked or are now working are concentrated in the most unfavorable occupations, and 27 percent of welfare mothers have never been employed.

They are also more likely to be members of a minority race and, therefore, face economic discrimination. Finally, the structure of AFDC [the Aid to Families with Dependent Children program], puts severe limitations on their incentives to work and earn.[16]

Educational Status

There have been many problems for women seeking admission to vocational schools and to higher education—particularly, advanced and professional training. Women have not been admitted to vocational training programs in industry, or to law and medical schools, and, even when admitted, have been screened out through lack of financial aid, which has been given primarily to men. Women have constituted about 50 percent of high school graduates, but only about 40 percent of first-year college students. In 1970–71, 43 percent of those receiving bachelors' degrees were women, 40 percent received M.A. degrees, and 14.3 percent were awarded Ph. D.'s.[17] There is a steady increase in the number of women receiving B.A and higher degrees, in proportion both to the number of women in the population and to the total number receiving degrees. According to recent figures, women are staying in college at a steady rate from year to year, while men are dropping out at an increasing rate. It, thus, appears that women B.A. graduates may soon equal the number of male graduates.[18]

Equality Before the Law

While economic status has been measured statistically, by the federal government, and monitored by a number of other sources, the legal status of women defies similar classification. The need for an Equal Rights Amendment, which had received support from the more militant suffragists in 1923 shortly after the passage of the enfranchising amendment, became obscured in the minds of many for two chief reasons. The "instant equality" it promised appeared to threaten many women who believed that the law protected their right to be supported by their husbands. And, women in the labor movement knew that laws they had worked very hard to pass—laws that governed working conditions of women differently from men—would be declared null and void by passage of the amendment. Regardless of the view of groups supporting or opposing the ERA, there was little dispute that women were not equal before the law in 1973, any more than they had been in 1923.

Several legal experts have explored the question of the status of women in statutes and before the courts. Those that have tried to categorize legal discrimination have found that major areas of unequal treatment include property distribution, application of criminal law, and as a result of so-called protective labor legislation. Two professors of law from New York University found discrimination so pervasive, both in statutes and in judicial decisions, that it defied classification.

Male-dominated legislatures and courts have historically exhibited the belief that women generally are—and ought to be—confined to the social roles of homemaker, wife, and mother, and, gainfully employed (if at all) only in endeavors which comport with their assumed subservient, child-oriented and decorative characteristics. . . .[18]

The authors reported that many protective labor laws which had prevented women from participating in higher-paying occupations, or in those that required overtime, had been struck down. Courts had, in some instances, granted that constitutional questions were involved in statutes which discriminated on the basis of sex, but,

despite such holdings by a number of state and lower federal courts, opinions continue to appear in which both the result and the reasoning are virtually indistinguishable from those issued nearly a century ago.[20]

It was too soon, therefore, to celebrate a "clear trend toward judicial recognition of women's rights."

In general, bias against women which has resulted in their inferior legal status, is found in the following areas:

1. Those laws and judicial decisions which deny women equal economic opportunity. (Such laws primarily dictate "protective" working conditions for women, but they may also involve granting of credit, signing of contracts, etc.);
2. In criminal law, a pervading sociosexual double standard has provided, among other inequities, longer sentences for women found guilty of violating the same criminal statutes as men, made prostitution a criminal act for women but not for men, and required evidence to convict for rape, which is not required for any other type of assault;
3. Laws which regulate family relationships, for the most part after the dissolution of a marriage, have made women less equal in the way in which property has been divided, in their responsibility for children of a broken marriage, and in other ways.

Economic Discrimination

Laws protecting women in factories, and in unskilled jobs, became discriminatory in the face of a developing technology and more liberalized pay scales. Female subway attendants, as long ago as the early twenties in New York, had fought laws which prevented women from working at night. A trade union movement, which brought safer practices and better working conditions for both men and women, and a number of other factors, including passage of the anti-sex discrimination title of the Civil Rights Act of 1964, had made most protective laws vestigial remnants of another era by the early 1970s. Some still survived and made for economic inequality:

The uneven coverage, wide variation among states, proliferation of exceptions for jobs for which coverage seems most appropriate, and outright exclusion of women from many lucrative occupations, demonstrate a lack of protective function. The conclusion that the laws serve primarily as an excuse for employers and unions to keep women in lower paying jobs, or out of the labor force altogether, is supported by the increasing number of women's lawsuits challenging these restrictions.[21]

There is general agreement among legal experts that passage of the Equal Rights Amendment[22] would extend benefits now granted exclusively to women (extra rest periods and the like), to men. Laws excluding women from occupations, or which unequally restrict hours, would be invalidated; indeed, many have been already, by court decisions involving Title VII of the Civil Rights Act. The extent to which granting credit has discriminated against women is now under study,[23] but banks and lending companies have been frank to admit that married women of childbearing age are looked upon as poor risks and are not granted credit as easily as are men, no matter what their job circumstances. A variety of other practices discriminated against women in such matters as pensions, social security payments, signing contracts and leases, and the manner in which income taxes were levied. In the late sixties and early seventies, they were under piecemeal attack by federal agencies, state legislatures, the courts, and by pressure groups endeavoring to eliminate such discriminatory practices.

Criminal Law

The socio-sexual double standard behind those aspects of criminal law which discriminate against women for the most part concerns criminal punishment for prostitution and rape, and sentences given to women for offenses which are significantly different from those given to men. As the legal authority Leo Kanowitz has pointed out: "In most states, males cannot be punished directly for partronizing a prostitute," and, where there are laws which punish such activity, they are more often than not used "only as an inducement to the male to cooperate in convicting the woman." Those who argue that the activity of the woman is criminal, while that of the man is not, since it is not commercial, seem to overlook the fact that "female prostitutes simply could not exist without male customers."

If the progress that American law has made in the last two centuries in rejecting the theory of male superiority is to be completed, women should no longer bear the entire burden of an offense that involves both sexes. As proposed by Abraham Flexner, one of the early students of the problem, in 1914: "The stigma and consequence of crime must . . . be either removed from the woman or affixed to the man."[24]

Women's rights groups—in particular, the National Organization for Women, at its annual meeting in Washington, D.C. on February 17–18 of 1973—favored abolition of all laws regulating prostitution. Suggested model codes, however, still deal with the problem of prostitution by penalizing women guilty of such practices. At the same time, some model codes have identified persons guilty of prostitution as "he" or "she," thus widening culpability to include both sexes. The well-documented Yale Law Review article on "Equal Rights for Women," reported that passage of the ERA would mean that

Prostitution laws which penalize only the seller would be subject to judicial scrutiny as classifications which would fall more heavily on one sex than the other. . . . Reformed penal laws have already begun to regulate patrons as well as prostitutes.[25]

Indeterminate or unequal penalties for the same or similar offenses are part of state and local statutes in most parts of the country. In some states women receive longer sentences for drunkenness, robbery, and other offenses than do men. New York has a law for youthful offenders (establishing the PINS or Persons in Need of Supervision program), which provides for the incarceration of women declared incorrigible until they are twenty, while young incorrigible men cannot be held past the age of eighteen. This law is representative of statutes that

require or permit judges to place women in a separate correctional status in which the lengths of their sentences are determined not by the judge but by correctional authorities within the limits set by statute.[26]

These, and laws which provide longer sentences for women, have not been declared unconstitutional, because courts reasoned that legislatures could legitimately conclude that female criminals were basically different from male criminals, that perhaps they were more amenable to rehabilitation and reform.

Men have gone unpunished for murdering their wives' lovers on the grounds of justifiable homicide, while women enjoyed no similar leniency if they murdered their husbands' mistresses. Several states have statutes similar to New Mexico's where it may be shown as a complete defense that the homicide resulted from the person's use of deadly force upon another who was at the time of the homicide in the act of having sexual intercourse with the accused's wife.[27]

Sentences for rape, nominally very high in many states, have involved a two-sided version of the sexual double standard. Rape sentences are high, at least partly, because extra-marital sex is considered a breach of the moral code that applies only to women. They have been difficult to enforce on the other hand, because proof of rape has been made almost impossible in the courts. The implication has been that a woman who has managed to get herself involved with a man to the extent of being raped must somehow have encouraged him, known him before, or, having agreed to sexual intercourse, felt guilty afterwards and decided to make it appear that she was overcome by force. The "consent defense" has meant that a defendant in a rape case may plead that the victim consented and the burden is on the victim to prove that she did not consent (e.g., a person who has been robbed or assaulted does not have to prove that he or she did not consent to the theft or attack). In no other crime is this necessary.

Many commentators still are obsessed by the fear that innocent men are often convicted of rape due to the malice of "sick" women. . . . These fears are largely groundless. It is more likely that guilty assailants escape due to the reluctance of victims to report the crime, police and district attorneys to prosecute, and jurors to convict.[28]

Rape laws came under increasing attack in the late sixties and early seventies. Many victims of rape had hesitated to bring charges for fear of public humiliation. Reviews of rape laws, at a time when rapes were becoming more frequent, and sexual matters discussed with greater frankness in the media than previously, promised long overdue analyses of outmoded laws and criminal court procedures.

Marriage and Divorce

The succinct comment of the 1848 Seneca Falls Declaration—"He has made her, if married, in the eye of the law civilly dead"[29] still has weight when applied to such matters as division of property after marriage, restrictions on use of a woman's maiden name, choice of legal residence, etc. Such discriminatory laws have deprived women of equal status in a number of ways. If a woman cannot establish her own legal residence, for example, she may be deprived of her right to free or lowered tuition at state schools, to serve as an administrator of an estate, to vote, or to run for public office. Women lack the power to sue for compensation for consortium (services, including companionship and sexual relations with spouse), as another example, in the event of the accidental deaths of their husbands, while, in most states, husbands have the right to sue for compensatory damages in the event of the death or incapacity of their wives.

Statutes governing ownership of property by marriage partners, as well as the failure of the law to establish clear responsibilities of the husband to support his wife while married, have created problems for women. The "community property" states, as they have been called, because housewives resident in these states who do not have independent incomes hold a legal share in family property, discriminate against women. A law review article points out that

in all the community states, except Texas and Washington, the husband has power of attorney over the community property; and in some states he can assign, encumber or convey the property without his wife's consent.[30]

Under the common-law principles which guide distribution of property for married couples in the remaining forty-two states, each partner owns whatever property he or she earns. But injustices occur. If the husband is the only income producer, the property acquired during marriage belongs entirely to him. State laws have modified the stringent common-law principle, but limitations remain, as many widows have discovered. In some states, a married woman cannot sell even her own property without her husband's permission. And nowhere, of course, is the value of a housewife's labor considered property under the common-law rules which guide inheritance statutes and other laws determining the division of property. Nor have statutes or legal decisions determined the exact scope of the legal duty of a husband to provide for wife and children while the family is living together.

Contrary to popular belief, alimony is ordered by courts in only a small percentage of divorce cases. Alimony is not usually awarded without regard to the wife's ability to support herself. And, with respect to child support, "the data available indicate that payments generally are less than enough to furnish half of the support of the children." With the earnings of women averaging 60 percent of those of men, women who work to support their children are contributing, by and large, more than their proportionate share, even when fathers comply fully with awards. The Citizens' Advisory Committee points out:

Far from resulting in diminution of support rights for women and children, the equal rights amendment could very well result in greater rights. A case could be made under the equal rights amendment that courts must require divorced spouses to contribute in a fashion that would not leave the spouse with the children in a worse financial situation than the other spouse.[31]

A Constituency Responds

Increasing numbers of women discovered the reality of inequality—economic and legal—in the late sixties and early seventies. They experienced it in a variety of ways. Working women supporting families discovered inequality in paychecks when they compared them with those of men doing similar jobs. The first women to challenge this kind of discrimination under the Equal Pay Act became legendary. Word spread about the law among single women with children to support often faced with higher living costs than men whose wives stayed home and saved the cost of child care. Women who joined activist organizations were informed by newsletters of the latest developments in congressional and court action. Some joined special lobbying groups like the Women's Equity Action League, the National Organization for Women, or the National Women's Political Caucus. Even those women who belonged to the more traditional type of social or business club went to meetings where special speakers discussed sex discrimination. The Business and Professional Women's Clubs adopted women's equality as one of its lobbying efforts early in its history, and responded to the new interest by paying increased attention to the problem at the end of the sixties by supporting the Equal Rights Amendment, equal pay, and equal employment opportunity.

Even groups associated with religions which emphasized male dominance began to take an interest in the subject of sex discrimination. An organization calling itself "The Clearing House on Women's Issues" was created in early 1972 as a federation of groups like the National Councils of Jewish Women, of Catholic Women, and of Negro Women, representative members of the International Ladies Garment Workers Union and other unions, and "auxiliary" wives groups. They formed for "communication and common action on economic and educational issues as they affect women." Other groups, which had never before considered sex discrimination to be a priority item, began to review the subject at open meetings: (e.g., women bank employees, women members of the American Jewish Congress, organizations of secretaries).

Some, but far from all, of the women's organizations with either an old or new interest in women's rights issues, had had experience lobbying within the administration and the Congress in an effort to affect national policy on the status of women when President Nixon took office in 1969. A major reason for the failure to move together for particular women's rights issues had been a major split among women's groups. The existence of sex discrimination had been recognized by both professional women and those who took an interest, either as labor leaders or as social reformers, in the condition of working women since before World War I. Both groups had united to push for suffrage, with the more militant professional and educated women taking the lead, but after its passage they had divided completely on the issue of the passage of another amendment.

The first version of the Equal Rights Amendment, introduced in Congress in 1923, was resisted by labor women and the social reformers because they believed that women, for the foreseeable future, would have to be protected by laws which treated them differently from men in the job market. The small group of militant suffragists, aided by succeeding generations of professional women, lobbied for the ERA, while the larger groups, many of whom associated themselves with the Franklin D. Roosevelt administration, lobbied for equal pay legislation.

Laws passed by Congress and the executive orders signed by Presidents Kennedy and Johnson in the sixties were not, therefore, so much the product of intensified lobbying by a united women's movement as the somewhat uncertain development of national policy in response to the more frequently heard repetition of the original American commitment to equality for *all*. The Civil Rights Act of 1964, and the later executive orders outlawing sex discrimination among federal contractors and the federal government, were by-products of the move for equality for minorities.

Increased lobbying, the product of a number of factors, was quite evident from 1969 on. Enough pressure had built so that, when President Nixon took office, women in the Republican party were able to persuade the chief executive and his advisers to appoint a Task Force on Women's Rights and Responsibilities. Its twenty or so recommendations for action by the administration and the Congress became rallying cries for many different groups, including women in the Democratic party. As was discussed at the beginning of this chapter, certain goals were agreed upon, and intensive lobbying by a number of groups undertaken over particular issues: passage of the Equal Rights Amendment, development of guidelines for national executive orders and laws which had been in effect from the sixties on, as well as strengthening of other legislation.

The story of the reaction of the president to increasing demand by women's groups, frequently allied with those representing minorities and with organized labor, will be recounted in Chapter 2; of Congress in Chapter 3. The president did not carry out the steps urged by his task force. When Congress attempted to implement legislative suggestions, he fought them. Women's groups lobbied the President and various members of the administration during the first four Nixon years. Several of the more militant turned to the Democratic party and gave their support to George McGovern, particularly in the pre-Convention period. The story of Nixon policy on women's rights during the first Nixon administration was one of frustration for those women who followed the implementation of federal programs closely. The true nature and results of presidential failure to support equality for women were apparent to many. It is possible to document them—their documentation accounts for the failure of improved status for women during the period of 1969 to 1972.

2

The Nixon Administration and the Status of Women, 1969–1972

A number of federal programs designed to end sex discrimination were in progress when President Nixon took office in 1969. Almost all of the civil rights legislation of the sixties, including two executive orders, had been applied to discrimination against women, as well as against minorities. There were extensive weapons against employment discrimination, as the Civil Rights Commission pointed out:

Equal opportunity in employment is mandated by a host of federal enactments—statutes, judicial decisions interpreting the Constitution, and Executive orders and regulations. Taken together, they constitute a comprehensive ban on job discrimination, covering all Federal, State and local jobs and nearly all private employment. Almost any act of discrimination by a government or private employer violates some aspect of Federal law. [1]

All of the programs for women, however, were poorly equipped in funds and authority to deal with the demands of the burgeoning women's movement. As an increasing number of women began to take advantage of newly discovered remedies which would provide them with higher pay and benefits, weaknessess in many of the laws themselves, and, especially, in the administration of the laws by the Nixon administration, became apparent, with that of the Equal Pay Act a notable exception.

Women's Rights as a National Issue

By the end of the 1960s the United States had made a clear commitment to provide equal economic opportunity for a majority of working women. Federal programs ordinarily function in any or all of these areas: they offer financial assistance, provide services, carry on or support research, or enforce regulations. Helping women to achieve economic equality were programs enforcing equal employment opportunity, providing services to individuals or groups, and performing research on matters related to sex discrimination. Direct grants for research or for projects were handled through agencies that gave grants for a variety of purposes—it was difficult to tell exactly how many had been given for research on sex discrimination, but it was an insignificant amount in comparison with the total sum expended to aid social science or medical research. The government's grant-giving powers did influence policy on the status of women through the contract compliance executive order which required institutions and companies to provide equal employment opportunity for women and minorities.

19

All of the programs except two were by-products of the civil rights movement of the sixties. The Women's Bureau (1920) and the division in the Employment Standards Administration responsible for administering the Equal Pay Act (1963) had been supported by women's groups which were strongly pro-labor, most of whose members were opposed to the ERA and favored legislation which "protected" women workers.

In 1964, a Civil Rights Act was passed which outlawed sex discrimination in private employment, without exciting much interest among women's groups. Organizations long associated with the Women's Bureau, and the director of the bureau, opposed the new statute on the grounds that the addition of sex discrimination might well serve the purpose of conservative Congressmen who wanted to defeat the bill. Many of these groups opposed federal efforts to end sex discrimination in employment opportunity because they believed racial and sex discrimination needed to be dealt with differently, and separately. As participation in the labor force increased among women, however, the younger generations became more aware of the difficulties they faced in getting white-collar promotions or blue-collar craft jobs. Pressure built for increasing government intervention in the correction of sex discrimination. By 1969, a majority of women in the work force were covered by one or more federal programs designed to guarantee equal opportunity. But the power and funds granted to these programs were insufficient to meet the demand of their constituents, as became increasingly apparent during the first Nixon administration.

Coordination and Leadership from the White House

Once federal resources are committed to the attainment of a national goal, the administrative units created as a result of the commitment have, in terms of the model used in this analysis, a policy subsystem—a set of actors in government, from interest groups, in political parties, and within the media, with goals of their own related to the developing federal programs. These groups make specific requests for increased or improved activity on the part of the bureaus or agencies responsible for the programs. If requests are not, or cannot be, fulfilled, they express their demands to the president, Congress, or, on occasions, to the courts. Women's groups, with very few exceptions, found the "output" of antidiscrimination programs inadequate, and put pressure first on the president, and then on Congress, to add resources to them. They began, in 1969, to translate broad goals into specific suggestions for the president and Congress, and to push with increasing intensity for them, in the time-honored fashion of interest groups in every major issue area.

The President

Presidents frequently find it expedient to respond to constituents by appointing commissions and task forces. As we have seen, both Presidents Kennedy and Nixon felt obliged to honor this custom, in response to demands from women involved in their campaigns and parties. Kennedy's commission, oriented toward the traditional trade union view, did not favor ERA and enforcement of equal employment opportunity in private employment, while advocating in a general fashion many of the goals still sought for women today—federally supported child care, social security payments that did not discriminate against wives or women workers, more appointments of women to policy positions in government, and so on. The Kennedy and Johnson administrations, in response, acknowledged some of the demands of women's groups: advisory and interdepartmental groups were formed, executive orders eventually signed, and some appointments made of women to policy positions.

President Nixon responded to demands from women in his party by appointing a task force to make recommendations on women's rights issues for the administration and for Congress. The Task Force report called for coordination from the top, for a female executive assistant in the White House who would "assume effective overall responsibility for federal legislative and executive action in the area of equal rights and responsibilities for women." It was also suggested that she should "chair the interdepartmental committee comprised of top level representatives and agencies with programs and functions significantly affecting women's rights and responsibilities."

The Interdepartmental Committee would review and coordinate Federal programs for the purpose of assessing their impact on women and girls and would recommend policies and programs to Federal agencies and to the President. It would oversee implementation of the President's program for equal opportunity in the Federal service.[2]

The president did not make such an appointment during his first term, nor did he arrange for a coordinating assignment in the White House to oversee federal policies in the area of women's rights. The president's equal opportunity program in federal government and in the private sector was, at best, a piecemeal affair, frequently at odds with the goals of the women's movement. The presidential appointment of Jacqueline Gutwillig, and the subsequent activities of the Citizens' Advisory Council on the Status of Women, filled some basic research needs on women's rights issues, but was a very minor reply to the major demands articulated by the President's Task Force. The council has published memoranda of a stimulating and provocative nature on various aspects of feminism, but since it has a paid staff of only two, its influence has been limited.[3]

The Office of Management and Budget, a reorganized version of the Bureau of the Budget designed to put the presidential arm to work as a management as well as fiscal aid, could have furthered the goals of equality for women. In March of 1971 on OMB memorandum was circulated, instructing examiners and management staff to include the monitoring of civil rights-oriented functions of bureaus throughout the federal government as part of their duties. The "Examiners' Handbook" was revised to include guidance on the review of civil rights programs. A special analysis of the budget was planned which would evaluate the ways in which federal funds were being used for all such programs (including those designed to end sex discrimination). A civil rights unit was established in OMB in the late spring of 1971; two years later, however, there was still an unfilled vacancy within its staff of two. The Civil Rights Commission pointed out, in a 1971 report,[4] that the effectiveness of the coordination of discrimination programs was blunted by its confinement to the budget, rather than to the management division.

The first Nixon administration failed to use still another possible coordinating device—the invocation of the attorney general's role as chief litigator of the federal government. The Department of Justice is supposed to function as the overseer of the enforcement phases of the federal equal opportunity program. The Nixon Task Force on Women's Rights and Responsibilities expressed disappointment in the Justice Department's fulfillment of its role. The 1969-1972 record of the Department would not have changed its judgment.

Although the Justice Department has participated in more than 40 cases of racial bias, it has not intervened on behalf of an individual discriminated against because of sex, except in one case on a procedural point.

The Justice Department, likewise, has not given aid in any case in which women are challenging the constitutionality of State laws discriminating on the basis of sex—with one exception in which race discrimination was also a factor.[5]

The task force recommended that the department seek "early and definitive court pronouncement" of the validity under the Fifth and Fourteenth Amendments of laws and practices which discriminated against women. It has not. As the agency of last resort when failure to comply with anti-discrimination regulations was proven and no sanction available to federal agencies, the Justice Department failed to function on behalf of equal rights for women during the first Nixon administration.

All but one or two of the task force's recommendations were ignored by President Nixon. He did not add his personal endorsement to the goals they outlined. He failed to call a White House Conference on Women's Rights and Responsibilities in 1970, as the task force had suggested, to commemorate the fiftieth anniversary of the suffrage amendment and the establishment of the Women's Bureau. Nor did his appointees in the Justice and Labor Departments, or any other department or agency, respond in the swift and firm manner called for by the report to demonstrate that they were "as seriously concerned with sex discrimination as race discrimination and with women in poverty as men in poverty."[6] His appointments of women to policy positions in the federal government lagged far behind those of his predecessor, with the number of women in GS-16 and above falling sharply during the first two years of his administration. The appointment of Barbara Franklin to a recruiting position in the White House, in April 1971, was the first public response the president made to women within his own party who were pressuring for fulfillment of the task force's recommendations. A few appointments were made, but by the end of 1972 only slightly more than 1 percent of policy positions were filled by women. In use of his other powers, the president also scored badly in terms of his task force's report. He opposed, in one way or another, much of the legislation it recommended. Legislation on the books was not implemented, as the following review of federal programs will show.

Federal Programs and Women's Rights, 1969-1972

The Women's Bureau

The combined histories of the Women's Bureau and the drive by the post-suffragist feminists to pass the ERA tell a great deal about the development of national policy on the status of women from 1920 to 1970. The Women's Bureau had its own set of constituents, social reformers with labor-oriented backgrounds, who took a limited view of the Seneca Falls goal of full legal and economic equality. The bureau lobbied mightily for protective legislation in the states, producing lengthy reports on working conditions which they believed to be unfair, unsafe, and unhealthy for women. They were not about to endorse an amendment which would, overnight, obliterate the fruits of their labor. From a stormy meeting in 1923 until the end of the sixties, the two groups of feminists—hard-core, militant pro-ERA activists on the one hand, and the "social feminists" on the other—found they had very little in common, as they pressured for separate legislative goals. The latter were in charge at the Women's Bureau, oriented toward the policies of organized labor, until the sex discrimination clause of Title VII of the Civil Rights Act of 1964 nullified protective state laws, and a revolution in attitudes toward the participation of women in the labor force made them useless.

The bureau's concentration on only one phase of its legislative mandate obscured its other functions. It was intended to serve "as the focal point of informed concern, policy advice, and leadership, and [be] the clearinghouse and central source of information within the federal government on questions relating to development of womanpower resources and the *economic, legal, and civil status of women.*"[7] (Emphasis added.) With a wider outlook, it is possible that the bureau might have related sooner than it did to other major problems confronting women. A larger constituency might have meant increased power and budget. As it was, the bureau was funded at about the same level in real-dollar terms throughout its existence.

When Elizabeth Koontz took over the leadership of the bureau during the first Nixon administration (her resignation was accepted by the president during the reorganization period of his second administration), she brought a background different from those of previous directors. Neither a social welfare nor labor person, she had been a teacher and former president of the

National Education Association. She favored the Equal Rights Amendment and declared that she thought the bureau should serve "as a catalyst for action . . . moving toward . . . specific goals," which included aiding impoverished women to obtain job training, the establishment of day-care facilities, and restructuring the "entire household industry."[8] Support from the president for the strengthening of the bureau and its resources was lacking, however. When Esther Peterson had served as bureau director, during the Kennedy-Johnson years, she had also been named Assistant Secretary for Labor Standards. Elizabeth Koontz did not receive an equivalent appointment. Her highest appointment was as Deputy Assistant Secretary for the Employment Standards Administration, which she received in April of 1972. The bureau had been downgraded from its original status for a period of several years. Since its inclusion with other divisions related to employment standards (not really similar in concern with that of the Women's Bureau), it has been somewhat more difficult to identify its goals and follow its functions. Elizabeth Koontz sought, unsuccessfully, a larger mandate and budget for the bureau.

Leaders of women's rights groups, were surprised when she chose to speak for the administration, in opposition to the extension of the Equal Pay Act to administrative, executive, and professional employees, urging that women in these occupational categories be covered by Title VII only. During testimony before the subcommittee chaired by Congresswoman Edith Green (D., Ore.) in June 1970 (a special subcommittee on education, of the House Committee on Education and Labor), she urged that supervision of sex discrimination programs in the federal government be added to the jurisdiction of the Women's Bureau rather than the Civil Rights Commission, as proposed by the Green legislation. She suggested that "this responsibility be placed in the Women's Bureau where it can be discharged together with other duties pertaining to the welfare of women."

We like to think that after 50 years of faithful stewardship in the realm of women's protection and women's advancement, the Women's Bureau might reasonably anticipate having the express blessing of Congress to put out some new shoots. The Bureau needs clear-cut authority to bring its functions up to date, to include such important matters as discrimination on the basis of sex.

Congresswoman Green, expressing a view that was shared by many leaders of women's rights groups, thought the idea of adding either investigatory or enforcement powers to the Women's Bureau "discriminatory." "Congress would give you about one-fiftieth of the amount of money they would give the other agencies. . . . It seems to me we ought to come to a time when we treat all women as human beings. . . ."[9] Virginia Allan, who had headed the Task Force on Women's Rights and Responsibilities, disagreed with Elizabeth Koontz, and favored both the extension of the Equal Pay Act and the addition of sex discrimination to the jurisdiction of the Civil Rights Commission.[10]

All in all, the Women's Bureau has lost more than it has gained in recent years. In 1970 all six divisions within a newly created Workplace Standards Administration (renamed Employment Standards), which included not only "programs for women," or the Women's Bureau, but contract compliance, wage and hour, occupational safety and health, wage determination for public construction, and federal employees' compensation programs were "consolidated" for the purposes of staff support and were required to report through a common regional director.[11] Staff members and some women's groups complained that the net effect was to reduce personnel available for Women's Bureau's duties, and the services it was supposed to make available to the public.

Programs Enforcing Equal Opportunity

All of the programs designed to enforce equal opportunity had been inspired, originally, by advocates of civil and economic rights for minorities, rather than by feminists. The exception was the Equal Pay Act, which had been passed in 1963 after two decades of pressure by women in the labor movement, as well as other women's groups. Because they lacked full authority and full coverage, the programs except for administration of the Equal Pay Act were inadequate in the ways in which they dealt with the problem of inequality in wages and employment opportunity. None of the statutes covered all women in the labor force; those women who were covered, and who tried to complain under the law, faced confusion and delays. The government was slow to issue guidelines, and complaints were backlogged because of insufficient personnel and a lack of sympathy on the part of staff members. The statutes themselves, and the executive orders which Presidents Johnson and Nixon had issued to foster equal opportunity, were generally low in enforcement power. Federal administrative procedures ordinarily vary from mild efforts (investigation and conciliation), to moderate (agency can bring suit), to strong (agency can issue cease and desist orders). Two of the federal programs—contract compliance and the employment program within the government—were the result of executive orders. A review of these programs shows that their weaknesses were the product of inadequate enforcement authority and the low priority assigned to them by the administration.

Equal Pay Act

"Equal pay for comparable work," guarantees that a woman, whose work requires as much skill and effort as that accomplished by a man, will receive equal compensation. The concept had the support of a wide range of women's groups during the forties and fifties. Supporters included women who had played leading roles in the labor and consumer movements, as well as groups which had begun to form in the early twenties among women in business and the professions. It was the single issue which bridged the gap between militant feminists supporting the ERA and those in the social welfare movement who opposed it. Opposition to the Equal Pay Act had come from an expected source—that is, by industries, represented by the National Association of Manufacturers, and by large companies which employed numbers of women, such as the General Electric Company. Despite the apparent unanimity when the bill was reconsidered in the early sixties, (the chairman of the subcommittee at 1961 hearings declared that not a single person or group could be found to testify against it), the bill that passed was a compromise and not entirely what its supporters had asked for.[12]

It passed as an amendment to the Fair Labor Standards Act (minimum wage), which limited its coverage far more than its supporters had wanted. And it called for equal pay for equal, rather than comparable, work, which supporters feared would seriously limit its effectiveness. The effect of the bill for working women in essence was as follows:

An employer having such employees [those covered by the Fair Labor Standards Act] may not discriminate on the basis of sex within an establishment by paying an employee of one sex at a lower rate than he pays an employee of the opposite sex for doing equal work on jobs requiring equal skill, effort, and responsibility which are performed under similar working conditions.[13]

About 61 percent of all wage and salary earners were covered by the amendments. Despite its limited coverage, the Equal Pay Act inherited enforcement features that were to make its administration more effective than other anti-sex-discrimination legislation proved to be. It provides anonymity to complaints, as well as speedy handling of their complaints.

In most instances employers correct violations disclosed by investigations conducted by Wage and Hour Compliance Officers without court action being necessary. In part, this is attributable to the widespread recognition of the fact that administrative efforts to secure voluntary compliance are supported by a vigorous litigation program. Even so, it is necessary in some instances to initiate court action in order to secure correction of violative pay practices.[14]

Since June, 1964, when the act became effective, through the end of June 1972, investigations have disclosed underpayments resulting from sex-based discrimination of almost $50 million owed to more than 100,000 employees.

Part of the effectiveness of the act has come from educational campaigns among employers. Investigation may be followed by guidance programs designed to correct company-wide discriminatory practices. In addition, most court decisions have been favorable to the Labor Department. Interpretations by courts have reinforced guidelines which have been generous in their elaboration of the original law. One of the more famous cases, brought against the Wheaton Glass Company, was the first Equal Pay case to reach the Supreme Court. An appellate court had ordered a total of more than $900,000 (including an award of interest at 6 percent), and was upheld in its decision by the high court when it denied *certiorari* (May 1970). Its most significant determination was that work needed only to be "substantially" equal to qualify for equal pay. Men performed some sixteen different tasks that women employees did not, but the court nevertheless decided that their jobs qualified as "equal" under the terms of the act.[15]

In general, the courts have been liberal in their interpretations of the act. Differentials in pay have not been justified, for example, on the basis that women, as a group, differ from men, as a group, in their qualification for jobs. Arguments that women cannot lift heavy objects continuously, in the same manner as men, or that they cost more to employ than men, do not substantiate valid exceptions to the act. Women workers may qualify for equal pay, if they are performing substantially equal tasks, and yet decline to perform certain incidental tasks that they may consider too physically difficult. As a further point, past history of sex discrimination is considered in determining whether there is a violation. If wage differentials are paid because of a training program, which has been denied to women, the company is in violation. The act also applies if women are employed to do substantially the same work that men *formerly* did, but are paid less than they were. The courts, in general, have taken a broader view of the term "equal work" than did the Labor Department itself initially. They are also adding interest to back payments—more than the department anticipated.

Administration of the Equal Pay Act has, by far, the best track record of any of the programs for women. Its backlog of cases is minimal, and faster techniques (using informal conferences with employers) reduced backlogs so that they were 28 percent lower in 1972 than they had been in 1971.[16]

Despite measurable gains in the handling of equal pay complaints, interested observers familiar with overall statistics provided by the Bureau of the Census were still aware of continued disparity between men and women workers in occupations requiring the same skills and effort. Administration of the Equal Pay Act, over an eight year period, had not budged the median rate of pay for women in comparison with that of men. The gap may be explained in part by the fact that until late 1972 more than 40 percent of women in the work force were not covered by the act. In 1969, 45.4 million employees were covered, of whom 17.1 million were women. As a result of the expansion of coverage in 1972, an additional 15 million employees were covered, including some 4 to 5 million women. Of equal, perhaps even greater, significance is the pattern of job classification and training that is imbedded in personnel management practices, which differentiate between male and female types of employment in ways that are only beginning to feel the effects of legislation. Unnecessary categorization of "male" and "female" jobs by industries is a classic example. There are, of course, cultural forces at work in early childhood and school experiences that have resisted change.

The Federal Government—Showcase Employer?

Since 1967 sex discrimination in federal employment has been forbidden, and equal employment opportunity mandated at all levels. At the very beginning of his first administration, President Nixon sent a memorandum to heads of departments and agencies reaffirming the national commitment to equal opportunity in the federal service. The chairman of the Civil Service Commission, Robert E. Hampton, was directed to review these efforts and to make recommendations for policy and program changes. In his reply to the president's request, the chairman noted that:

Despite significant gains in overall employment of minority group persons in the Federal service, too many of our minority employees are concentrated at the lower grade levels, victims of inadequate education and past discrimination. Our women employees are also largely concentrated in the lower grade levels.[17]

These were challenges, the chairman stated, that "dictated some forthright program changes."

Under Executive Order 11478 (signed in August 1969), which constituted the president's reply to Hampton's request for presidential action, equal opportunity for women at every level of federal service was to be part of major national policy. A three-pronged program was established, under the direction of the Civil Service Commission.

1. A legal, regulatory, and administrative framework to carry on the purpose of full equality of opportunity was created;
2. Practice was to be brought "in closer accord with merit principles through the elimination of attitudes, customs, and habits which have previously denied women entry into certain occupations, as well as higher level positions throughout the career services . . . .";
3. Women were to be encouraged to "compete in examinations for federal employment and to participate in training programs leading to advancement."[18]

Agency directors and department heads were told to incorporate the newly designated Federal Women's Program into their overall equal employment opportunity programs, which had been functioning on behalf of minorities since 1965. Several specific requirements were outlined for program coordinators to fulfill in recruiting, hiring, and promotion procedures. The key of effective EEO and affirmative action was, the report declared, "the individual supervisor." For evaluation purposes, by agency as well as the commission, departments and agencies were to maintain certain data (particularly the number of women in relation to the total number of employees at each grade level) on data processing equipment to "assist in program management." Three criteria for evaluation purposes were set:

1. Adequate upward mobility programs in all agencies and departments;
2. Swift and fair grievance procedures to process discrimination complaints in all agencies and departments;
3. Full support from the president and top policy officials, accompanied by a significant increase in appointments of women to high level federal positions.[19]

In a memorandum sent in May 1971 to all department and agency heads, it was requested that specific goals be set for increased employment of women at the GS-13 to -15 levels.

Evaluation of Federal Women's Program

The Director of the Federal Women's Program, Helene Markoff, criticized the program in very frank terms in the Spring 1972 issue of the Public Administration Review:

In spite of the breakthrough appointments and in spite of the growth in Federal Service Entrance Examination statistics, federal policy of equal opportunity for women has not yet become practice. In many areas the FWP is ignored, overlooked, or dismissed with ridicule. It does not have a high priority rating with many installations and with many administrators. An activity may be aggressively pursuing equal opportunity for minority groups . . . and at the same time overlooking equal opportunity for women.[20]

Several factors have been cited as contributing to the failure of the Federal Women's Program to show even small increases in the number of women employed at GS-9 and above. Daisy Fields, a career civil service employee for several years, and formerly an assistant in the program, has criticized the failure of the government to produce statistics on the number of women employed in the government, despite provisions for this in government directives:

The reason for collecting statistics, for example, is to enable the Commission to monitor the Women's Program to ensure that its policies are being carried out. Yet the Commission appears to be unable to accord this information requirement high enough priority to turn out data with a time frame that would make it useful.[21]

The principle of "accountability" for affirmative action programs depends on the speed with which statistics can be obtained and the success of the implementation of the program judged. The federal government is supposed to evaluate affirmative action plans for private industry and institutions of higher education, and to call them to account if they are not functioning; it is difficult to see how it can supervise the accountability functions of other programs if it is not providing leadership within the government. Federal employment statistics for October 1970 were not issued until December 1971, although data processing would have permitted almost instant reproduction. The 1971 data was not released until April 1973, and, then, in a form which made comparisons difficult. Data for 1972 has been promised. It will be in the same form as previous years, but full reports for 1971 are lost forever, according to the Civil Service Commission.

Federally Employed Women, an association representing women in the federal government, conducted a survey of the Federal Women's Program in the spring of 1972. A questionnaire was sent to all agencies asking a number of questions about their federal women's program, and for figures on their goals and timetables for promoting women to the GS-13 through -15 categories. Only seven agencies and three departments indicated that they had set any goals at all. The Labor Department, which houses three programs designed to assist the nationwide effort to end sex discrimination, had few women in top level positions, and set goals only for its GS-16 through -18 positions (its 1973 goal for these positions was to increase the number of women in these positions, from 8 to 15 out of 140). Despite an increase in total number of GS-13 through -15 positions from 3,119 in October 1971 to 3,258 in March 1972, the number of women employed at these levels had actually declined from 408 to 386.[22] A report by an in-agency task force, which was described in the *New York Times* in September 1972, was critical of Labor Department policies toward women and minorities. It charged that "negligible efforts had been made by the department to recruit minorities and women for executive and midlevel positions." In reply, the department said that it was developing an affirmative action program for fiscal year 1973, although this was already five years after the first promotion policies were established.[23]

Other federal agencies whose missions emphasized equal opportunity, the EEOC, and the Civil Service Commission, also revealed inadequacies in establishing vigorous promotion policies for women:

Notable exceptions to agency reports [i.e., they did not reply], include the Equal Employment Opportunity Commission, despite the obvious connection between overall agency mission and internal employment practices. The Civil Service Commission letter confuses CSC's institutional responsibilities with their responsibilities as an employer.... The White House also failed in their [sic] capacity as an employer—in addition to their roles as the initiator of the Executive Order prohibiting discrimination. FEW members agree that agencies with government-wide EEO responsibilities should practice what they preach and should be the first agencies willing to report with respect to their own internal personnel practices.[24]

Reasons given by at least one agency for not employing women at a higher level were counter to legal practice. The National Credit Union Administration said women were not hired as examiners because,

Examiners are required to travel extensively within an assigned area, and are away from home about 40-70 percent of the time. This fact, plus the necessity of having to handcarry a typewriter and an adding machine to each work location, has resulted in NCUA's current employment of only 4 [out of 340] women examiners.[25]

A Nader report confirmed the judgments FEW made about the government's EEO program. It called the operative programs

a patchwork fashioned more with a view toward "image" or public relations impact than efficacy in the attainment of minority group and female employment and promotion.[26]

As far back as January 1968, the Federal Personnel Manual was revised to include specific suggestions for ways in which agency heads could provide and evaluate "measurable progress" in bringing about the end of minority and sexist discrimination in the federal service. The results, until 1972, have been summed up by the report as follows:

The Bureau of Personnel Management Evaluations [in the Civil Service Commission] refuses to make available to the public its evaluation of agencies' EEO programs. . . . The Commission has developed Guidelines for Agency Self-Evaluation of EEO programs. . . . Helpful guidelines they may be; enforcement they are not.[27]

The FEW report showed Federal Women's Programs in most of the agencies to be erratically and poorly staffed. Neither Commerce, with 30,308 employees, nor Interior, with over 51,000, had full-time program coordinators; nor did the Veterans Administration, with 117,750 employees.[28]

Criticism of Grievance Procedure

The Civil Service Commission complaint procedure for those employees who believe they have been victims of sex or minority discrimination has been criticized by the Nader investigator, as well as the House Committee on Education and Labor. The latter referred to the "critical defect" of the federal EEO program as the "failure of the complaint process". Mary Eastwood, former Justice Department attorney and an expert in complaint procedures, believed that the weaknesses of EEO procedures outweighed its strong points. The time given to the complainant to file—15 days—was "not very long for an employee or applicant to make a decision on whether to take on an employer or prospective employer, especially if it is the federal government."[29] It compares unfavorably with the 90 days given employees in private employment, and the 180 days granted under contract compliance procedures. Appeals from agency decisions could be taken to the Board of Appeals and Review of the Civil Service Commission for a final decision. This procedure was revised as a result of legislation passed in 1972 (see chapter 3).

Mary Eastwood's criticism, also noted by the House subcommittee, was reaffirmed by the Nader investigation cited above. It pointed out that:

unlike some other federal programs, there is no doubt whatsoever about the adequacy of the Commission's authority to do its job. It has ample authority, leverage and disciplinary power vis-à-vis other federal agencies, but it has been reluctant to use these tools.

Calling the disciplinary actions pursued by the commission a "tragic farce," the report accused the commission of pursuing "reluctance"

... by delegation of responsibilities to the subject agencies and by knowingly diffuse lines of administrative authority and control within the Commission to enforce the Federal EEO Program [in such a way] that a deliberateness of non-enforcement and de facto repudiation of the program prevail.[30]

The Nader report cites delays in handling grievance procedures, which occur despite time limits set by the program. The final recourse for repeal, the Board of Appeals and Review, has had a heavy backlog of cases for both minorities and women. Very rarely have complainants been granted promotions as the result of appeals—once in 1969, of 150 appeals; twice in 1970, of 180 appeals; and five times in 1971, of 174 appeals.

The commission was also criticized for the ways in which its implementation of grievance procedure had failed to develop a systematized body of law, rules, criteria, or guidelines for the evaluation of the merits of a discrimination complaint.

Unchanneled discretion is allowed in deciding every complaint, and administrative rules to prevent arbitrary and capricious decisions are nonexistent . . . [BAR] decides each case on an ad hoc basis, takes four to six months to decide an appeal and in 1970 reversed an agency head's decision on an EEO complaint in only 1.4 per cent of the EEO appeals before it—5 reversals out of 368 complaints reviewed . . . .[31]

The Results—The Statistics on Employment of Women

The Civil Service Commission has responsibility for providing accurate data on the number of women employed at each pay grade level in every department and agency in the federal government. As indicated above, figures that would permit comparison with previous years were not released for 1971. The commission, through Helene Markoff, director of the Federal Women's Program, denies that complete figures are available for that year because statistics on male-female employment for agencies with fewer than 2,500 employees were not collected.[32] They have been for 1972, however, and will be available in the future. In lieu of full statistics for 1971, partial statistics were produced which makes comparison difficult. It is quite clear, however, that the EEO program for women was ineffective at all levels, in all agencies, during the entire time of the first Nixon administration.

Claims by the president himself, and by Barbara Franklin, assistant to the president for female executive recruitment in 1971-72, that "significant corners" had been turned or "breakthroughs achieved" in the employment of women at the supergrade level are not substantiated by government sources. The president was quoted in March, 1973, as saying that his administration had "quadrupled the number of women in high government posts" during his first four years in office. Barbara Franklin declared that there had only been 26 women in such positions in 1969—(a drop from a previous statement that there were 36).[33] There had been far more than 36 women in such positions in 1968 or 1969, according to Civil Service Commission figures. In 1968, there were more than 147 in GS-16 and above according to the Commission. The number of women in grade levels above 18 has, according to

Commission figures, actually decreased from 1969, when it was 17, to 10 in 1970, and to 6 in 1971.

One possible source of confusion is the type of appointment among the 117 claimed to have been made in the twelve months prior to the fall of 1972. If they are all policy appointments to GS level 16 and above, their names are not included in the official Civil Service list of such appointments. There are actually 57 women's names listed as policy appointees in GS-16 and above; If Barbara Franklin was referring to advisory committee members serving without pay or on per-diem she does not say so. In any event, if that is the case, the comparison with previous administrations is unfair. In the Senate Committee's list for 1968, there was a total of 40 women listed in GS-16 and above, excluding women serving without compensation, or on a per-diem basis. Although figures for 1972 had not been released for publication when this book went to press, the expectation was that no increase would be shown in the number of GS-16 and above, regardless of whether the appointment was career or political.

Total number of employees, number and percentage of women employees in pay grade levels 13 and above, 1969-1971[34]

Pay grade Level	1969			1970			1971		
	Total	Women	Percent	Total	Women	Percent	Total	Women	Percent
GS-13	98,667	4,290	4.3	97,553	4,376	4.5	102,641	4,683	4.6
GS-14	49,127	1,889	3.8	47,873	1,705	3.6	50,274	1,907	3.8
GS-15	26,418	717	2.7	26,655	886	3.3	27,160	835	3.1
GS-16	6,344	115	1.8	5,201	92	1.8	5,812	89	1.5
GS-17	2,498	37	1.5	2,353	28	1.2	2,418	27	1.1
GS-18*	700	4	.6	442	5	1.1	998	10	1.0
above 18	656	17	2.6	1,099	10	.9	338	6	1.8

* The difference in figures for 1971 in GS-18 and above are accounted for by a "reevaluation" in policy appointment pay by the Nixon administration.

Federal Contract Compliance-Department of Labor

The federal program which guides firms with government contracts in equal employment opportunity, was begun as presidential effort to initiate policy in the face of Congressional failures to agree on a statute to end discrimination in employment. As tools to limit discrimination (in origin, related to blacks and other minorities, but not to women), executive orders compelling fair employment practices by firms with government contracts have been issued by six presidents, beginning with Franklin D. Roosevelt in the early 1940s. The Kennedy commission had proposed a separate executive order which would apply to woman and would merely encourage rather than enforce a prohibition against discriminatory practices.

When Lyndon Johnson signed EO 11246 in 1965, requiring companies with federal contracts to take "affirmative action" to insure equal opportunity, the new and more positive approach embodied in the EO was not extended to women. After prodding from many women's groups, the Interdepartmental Committee on the Status of Women (established in 1963, as recommended by the Kennedy commission) eventually suggested that sex discrimination be added to proscribed practices. Under EO 11375, sex discrimination was forbidden in October of 1967; its administration has been under the guidance of the Office of Federal Contract Compliance in the Labor Department.[35] The EO covers firms with contracts of more than $10,000, those with contracts of more than $50,000 are required to develop *written* affirmative action plans to provide equal opportunity to minorities and women. The Labor Department has been delegated authority to implement the order as it applies to some "compliance" agencies which, in turn, surpervise the order for general types of contracts, even if they have not granted them.

The Nixon Task Force on Women's Rights and Responsibilities, responding to the criticisms women's groups and others had made of Labor Department failure to issue guidelines for contract companies to follow, urged that the secretary "immediately issue guidelines to carry out the prohibition against sex discrimination in employment by government contractors, which was added to Executive Order 11246 in October 1967, became effective October 28, 1968, but remains unimplemented."[36] Written guidelines were issued on January 30, 1970, but they did not apply to sex discrimination. Whether they did or not was unclear at first, but it was confirmed by the director of the Office of Federal Contract Compliance, somewhat later, that they did not. Thr procedures, one critic has pointed out, "for determining underutilization are not entirely appropriate to meet the more difficult and elusive problems of sex discrimination because of differences in work force patterns and participation rates in the labor force and certain occupations. For women, the Labor Department regulations contained a gentle statement that employers 'shall take affirmative action to recruit women to apply for those jobs where they have been previously excluded'."[37] The Secretary of Labor in July 1970, acknowledging that there should be specific guidelines that applied to sex discrimination, said that consultations with private groups would soon begin. In January of 1971, preparations began and, in late April, consultations were underway. In December 1971, the regulations were issued as "Revised Order No. 4," to become effective four months later.

Doris Wooten, who is Assistant Director of the Office of Plans, Policy, and Programs of the Office of FCC, writing in the fall of 1972, acknowledged that the sex discrimination phase of the contract compliance program had not been launched until near the end of the first Nixon administration. She provided, in summary form, the "ingredients" of an affirmative action plan for private industry, in keeping with the policies finally determined by the Labor Department.

1. A self-analysis of deficiencies in the contractor's compliance posture, including a utilization analysis to determine whether minorities and women are being under-utilized in one or more job classifications;
2. Corrective action designed to remedy deficiencies;

3. Goals and timetables, where number or percentages are relevant in developing corrective action;
4. Development of reaffirmation of any equal opportunity policy;
5. Means of disseminating the policy both within the establishment and throughout the community;
6. Means of formulating and implementing internal reporting systems to measure the program's effectiveness;
7. Procedures for obtaining active support of local and national groups designed to improve employment.

The guidelines prevented contractors from advertising under separate male and female classifications, basing seniority lists on sex, making distinctions between married and unmarried persons by sex, or penalizing women because they required leave for childbirth. Women must not only be granted leave of absence for childbearing, but also be reinstated to their original jobs or to positions of like status and pay following childbirth.[38]

Definitions of "underutilization," part of the "goals and timetables heart" of affirmative action planning, emphasize that women and minorities are considered underutilized in any job category in which there are fewer than "would reasonably be expected by their availability." It is assumed that minorities are seeking employment in equal proportion to their number in the population. Such an assumption, however, is not made for the employment of women. Rather, the availability of women *seeking* employment is used as a criterion. Contractors have been directed to give special attention to the utilization of women in such categories as officials, managers, professionals, technicians, nonretail sales workers, and blue-collar craftsmen.

The Civil Rights Commission, echoing the criticism of many minority and women's groups, focused sharp criticism on the OFCC's performance during the first Nixon administration.

OFCC has not yet provided Federal agencies (a January 1973 report stated) with adequate mechanisms for resolving compliance problems, thus weakening the impact of these agencies upon employment discrimination. The Department of Labor has not given the necessary impetus to implement the Federal contract compliance program effectively. It has delayed the approval of OFCC policy directives which would help provide essential guidance and leadership to agencies with compliance responsibilities.[39]

CRC criticized the reorganization which had placed OFCC in the Employment Standards Administration; it favored placing the contract compliance functions in the Equal Employment Opportunity Commission. The commission was not satisfied that "Order No. 14," implemented in July 1972, which was designed to tighten and improve affirmative action plans, was sufficient to accomplish its purpose, and complained that several other directives standardizing compliance procedures had been delayed in publication. Order No. 14 specified that affirmative action plans must include an analysis of the areas within which the contractor was deficient in the utilization of minority groups and women. It also provided that goals and timetables must be set for "good-faith" efforts to "create" such utilization at all levels and in "all segments" of the plant's work force. Contractors must send their written affirmative action plan in advance of a compliance review. If they do not, show cause orders will be issued. If the plan is considered to be inadequate, it must be corrected in 30 days; if it is still considered unsatisfactory, enforcement procedures under Order No. 4 will go into effect (delay or cancellation of the proposed contract). The effectiveness of OFCC's collection and review of data on the availability of minorities and women has also been criticized by CRC. It believed that OFCC's "ultimate goals" have not been made clear.

They [the contract agencies] have received insufficient instructions and guidance for the conduct of preaward and compliance reviews, for the collection and analysis of data, and for the evaluation of affirmative action plans.[40]

The contract compliance program, after a slow start, had not produced sufficient results for sound critical review in the limited time between implementation of Revised Order No. 4, in the spring of 1972, and the end of the first Nixon administration. Employers have been confused by the lack of guidelines, particularly with reference to the employment of women. There are numerous legal questions which have been raised by employees and contract companies, which have bogged down OFCC enforcement efforts. The Civil Rights Commission believes that the reorganization, which lowered the status of OFCC for the saving of several hundred thousand dollars, was not worth the "substantially weaker" program which resulted.

The saving should be weighed against the economic cost of discrimination in contract employment, which OFCC estimates to be $24 billion per year.

OFCC is guilty of inefficiency and sluggishness in carrying out the EO in other ways:

OMB authorized 112 positions for OFCC in Fiscal Year 1972, but the Department of Labor made no effort to fill many of these positions. Although it was intended that manpower should be transferred from ESA's Wage and Hour Division to fill many of these positions, this transfer never took place. In fact, some of the staff within the OFCC national office were transferred to other divisions in the Department. . . . ESA has requested $2.6 million for OFCC in Fiscal Year 1973. This is the same as the 1972 level, which has been inadequate for implementing a comprehensive contract compliance program.[41]

HEW's Office for Civil Rights

Supervision of the antidiscrimination executive order, as it related to educational institutions with government contracts, was delegated to the Department of Health, Education, and Welfare by the Department of Labor. The long delay in implementing a program, including guidelines and compliance reviews, that took place in OFCC itself was matched at HEW. Dr. Bernice Sandler, an officer in the Women's Equity Action League, who inspired the first use of the executive order by women at universities, has stated:

Until WEAL filed its charges [250 were filed in 1970 with HEW on behalf of women employed at the professional and staff levels in educational institutions] the Executive Order was not enforced with regard to sex by federal agencies.[42]

Neither HEW officials nor university administrators deny the statement. The long delay in implementation of the EO has been well documented. As Dr. Sandler pointed out in an article in April 1972: ". . . despite nearly two years of effort, institutions still have little guidance [from HEW] in approaching and resolving the issues that relate to contract compliance." Guidelines were not officially issued by HEW to the academic community until October 4, 1972, although the order had been in effect since 1968.[43]

During the period between the initial "discovery" of the order, as it related to discrimination against women faculty members and other employees of universities and colleges with federal contracts, and the eventual issuance of guidelines in mid-1972, compliance review procedures dealing with numerous complaints from women evolved in a hit-or-miss fashion. Understaffed (CRC reported in January 1972, that 8 staff members in Washington worked on EO 11246, and a total of 55 in regional offices), HEW soon experienced a backlog of complaints. Women on campuses, as well as college and university administrators, were highly critical not only of delays in reviewing complaints, but also of lack of system in HEW reviews. Legal questions arose, which further muddied compliance waters—regarding due process of law in HEW procedures—as to whether or not HEW had the power to compel payment of back pay after it had determined that a pattern of discrimination existed on a campus, as well as in other matters.

In general, the guidelines followed those established by OFCC's Revised Order No. 4. Educational institutions must prepare written affirmative action plans under the same terms as private companies. (While no record is kept of the number of institutions which have government contracts, more than a majority of the 2,500 institutions of higher learning do have such contracts.) Campuses with contracts of more than $1 million are subject to preaward compliance reviews. Such review will determine the efficacy of the affirmative action plan, which must contain several provisions:

1. A clearcut statement of equal opportunity policy;
2. Formal and informal dissemination of the policy;
3. Administrative procedures for its implementation;
4. Identification of "problem areas," including data gathering on the race, sex, color, religion, or national origin of employees and applicants for employment;

5. An internal auditing and reporting system, plus an annual formal report to OCR on the results of its affirmative action program;
6. Publication of affirmative action programs. Everything but confidential information about employees, trade secrets, and the like is available to the public;
7. OCR urges that "particular attention be given the need to bring into the deliberative and decision-making process those within the academic community who have a responsibility in personnel matters.[44]

The question of the desirability of "goals and timetables" has been raised by the American Jewish Committee, and other groups, who have accused some universities of denying jobs to qualified members of the latter group in favor of less well qualified blacks and women. A letter from President Nixon to the American Jewish Committee, sent in August of 1972, responded to a question about the imposition of "quotas" for employment of minorities and women in educational institutions:

With respect to these affirmative action programs, I agree that numerical goals, although an important and useful tool to measure progress which remedies the effect of past discrimination, must not be allowed to be applied in such a fashion as to, in fact, result in the imposition of quotas, nor should they be predicated upon or directed towards a concept of proportional representation.[45]

Federal policy was not redirected by the presidential letter, as a later article by J. Stanley Pottinger, director of OCR during the first Nixon administration, affirmed.

Pottinger believed that the complaint by the American Jewish Committee was the beginning of a "backlash" among white male administrators and professors, which had to have a "galvanizing symbol." He pointed out that the EO actually calls for the elimination of quotas restricting women and minorities, antinepotism policies, discriminatory recruitment procedures and the like, and substitutes goals commensurate with availability. The backlash came when OCR began to enforce the order:

When the Office made its presence on campus felt, however—by deferring payment of some $23 million in Federal contracts to various universities pending compliance with the order—it began to raise the academic community's eyebrows. Today a significant and vocal segment of that community is actively challenging HEW's enforcement of Executive Order 11246 and the policies upon which it is based.[46]

In any case, the shift to precontract compliance reviews, the possibility of delaying a contract via simple and effective procedures, more uniform guidelines for investigations, speed and diligence in completing reviews, promised effective implementation of the EO. Staff members pointed to the fact that they had had no increase in staff to help reduce the enormous backlog of campus complaints by women.[47] Vetoing of HEW's 1973 fiscal year budget had prevented a scheduled increase.

EEOC—The Primary Enforcement Agency

The major federal legal vehicle for enforcement of equal opportunity for women in private employment evolved into a complex schema of procedures and case law during the first Nixon administration. Title VII of the Civil Rights Act had been intended, by its creators and major supporters in the Kennedy-Johnson period, to deal with unfair racial and minority practices in private employment. As the legislative history shows, women prominent in the Kennedy administration opposed the addition of sex discrimination to prohibited practices. Regardless of the motives of the legislators, however, the act was to have a profound effect on the role of the working woman in the United States.

The important point is that for the first time in United States history, an authoritative national agency and the courts have been charged with the responsibility of developing viable equitable principles to govern the employment role of men and women in American society, and opposition to sex discrimination has become official national policy.[48]

Proponents of a national role on fair employment practice enforcement, opposed by a conservative coalition of Southern Democrats and Republicans, lost their effort to add the granting of cease and desist power to the 1964 Act and failed, even, to give the agency the power to bring suit against an employer. Such power, would have enabled the newly created Equal Employment Opportunity Commission to investigate and hear a complaint of discrimination, and, upon deciding that the employer was guilty of discrimination, to issue an order causing him to "cease and desist" from the discriminatory practice.

By the 1964 Act, discrimination for reasons of sex, race, color, religion, or national origin in hiring, promotion, firing, wages, testing, training, apprenticeship, and all other conditions of employment was illegal. Failure to provide support for EEOC in the form of funding and administrative power has, however, created a huge backlog of cases (some 53,000 as of June 30, 1972—about 25% of these related to sex discrimination, and a predicted rise to 70,000 cases was forecast for June 1973, with the percentage of new cases coming from women rising to over 40 percent).[49] Individual employees bringing charges have failed to receive prompt processing of their complaints. The limited coverage of the law—faculty and professional staffs of colleges and universities were not covered until March 1972, nor were state and local government employees, and employees and union members of companies and unions with fewer than 24 members—has seriously impaired its effectiveness. Because of EEOC's lack of enforcement power there was much pressure by civil rights and women's groups to revise EEOC's legislative mandate during the 92nd Congress.

Guidelines established by EEOC, and interpretations of them and the act, have for the most part found favor with groups fighting sex discrimination. The provision which would have denied women employees a job, if the position in question called for a male "bona fide occupational qualification" (known as a BFOQ), has been interpreted narrowly. Only a purpose related to "authenticity or genuineness" can determine such an exemption (e.g., the need to hire an actor or an actress for a part in a play). State protective laws limiting the working hours or the employment of women in "hazardous" occupations are considered to conflict with and to be superseded by the antidiscrimination clause of Title VII. The point has been summarized by Catherine East:

The thrust of the guidelines and Court decisions interpreting the BFOQ exceptions is that men and women applicants and employees cannot be considered or treated as a class. Each individual must be considered on his or her own merits. The BFOQ exception will so rarely be in order that the safest and most sensible course for employers to follow is to assume that *no job may be denied to all women or to all men.* (Emphasis in text.)[50]

Title VII, broader in scope and wider in coverage than either the Equal Pay Act or EO 11246, interrelates with both programs. Women who believe themselves to be discriminated against in many cases may appeal for remedy to any one or all three programs. Because of Title VII's broader jurisdictional provisions, EEOC has played a leadership role in curbing discriminatory practices in a number of areas, including coverage of dependents in insurance plans, differences in optional or compulsory retirement ages based on sex, differences in coverage of maternity benefits for wives of employees and for female employees, and provision for maternity benefits in insurance plans, as if pregnancy were a temporary disability. Interpretation of guidelines has resulted from suits brought by women, since the agency could only conciliate and could not file pattern or practice suits. Catherine East has commented on this aspect of EEOC activity in the years preceding the 1972 Act:

A surprisingly large number of suits were brought by women employees—almost entirely blue collar and low paid clerical employees—women of extraordinary courage, intelligence, and leadership, who have been isolated and harrassed in retribution. Several of the landmark decisions in the Circuit Courts of Appeals have been won by volunteer women attorneys. The dramatic story of these gallant women, the plaintiffs and the attorneys, will some day be written in full.[51]

Among significant court interpretations of the law have been the following:

1. Classification of jobs as "male" and "female," or in any other way ("light" and "heavy," if women are restricted to "light" jobs) are illegal;
2. Employers may not refuse to hire a women, or a man, based on assumptions regarding their comparative employment characteristics as women (or men) in general;
3. State laws prohibiting the employment of women in certain occupations, such as jobs requiring the lifting or carrying of weights exceeding

certain limits, or in jobs requiring night work, or for more than a specified number of hours, are in conflict with Title VII, and are illegal;

4. Ads for employment must not express a sex preference or be placed in columns headed "male" or "female";

5. Married or single women with children may not be excluded as a class from jobs, unless a similar policy is applied to male applicants.

Despite the favorable decisions which have provided large sums of back pay to thousands of women employees, and the promise of changed employment practices, criticism of EEOC operation has been severe. Mary Eastwood pointed out in December of 1971 that:

During the first five years of its existence, the EEOC found reason to believe discrimination existed in 63 percent of the charges investigated, but in less than half of these was it successful in achieving conciliation.[52]

She points out that some of EEOC's "failure rate" may have been due to lack of enforcement power. The Civil Rights Commission points to its lack of budget. The 1971 report said that "it had not had sufficient budget and staff resources to carry out its responsibilities with anything approaching maximum effectiveness." With almost a fourth of its complaints dealing with sex discrimination, its "resources have not been directed proportionately to the issues . . . its efforts to deal with sex discrimination continue to be on a complaint-oriented basis." The commission noted that EEOC employed no women at the supergrade level.[53] EEOC had restricted its enforcement role beyond the very limited one granted to it by Congress by adopting a passive role and placing too heavy an emphasis on the processing of individual discrimination complaints. It was accused of making little use of its initiatory capabilities, such as public hearing and commissioner-initiated charges.

The January 1973 report of the CRC, while still critical of EEOC operation, expressed the belief that "EEOC [was] just beginning to take a systematic approach to handling its responsibility." A priority system for handling complaints was being developed, but increased staff and reliance on such outside assistance as state fair-employment agencies was also needed. Training of employees needed to be better organized, and prompt attention given to the implementation of the 1972 EEOC Act.[54]

Other EEOC Functions

EEOC has research and service functions designed to contribute to its antidiscrimination goals. It collects reports, for example, from employers, local unions, and joint labor-management apprenticeship committees throughout the United States. All employers who have 100 or more employees on their rolls, and who are covered by Title VII or EO 11246, must file annual reports including detailed data on four minority groups (each divided by sex): Negroes, Spanish-surnamed Americans, Orientals, and American Indians. A model was developed to provide a method for identifying patterns of severe discrimination which enables EEOC and OFCC to target areas of greatest need and, thus, to maximize limited resources in appropriate areas. Measurements of minority employment thus devised are "being utilized . . . in a long-term project to identify the comparable advantage offered by alternative types of commission effort—specifically, the compliance process, hearings and industry meetings, and technical assistance." EEOC also has "cooperative relationships" with state and local equal employment opportunity agencies. By law it must defer cases to 35 states which have such agencies. (EEOC can receive cases after 60 days, however, if the complainant wishes.) EEOC has also assisted state and local agencies with grants and contracts, and has technical assistance to offer employers in developing affirmative action. It has held regional hearings which publicly reviewed employment opportunity within particular areas, with the object of following up with efforts to solve publicized problems.

Federal Programs–A Summary

All of the programs described above experienced increasing "stress" during the first Nixon administration. Continued disparity between income and opportunities available to women (both white and minority women), and to white men, despite a well publicized national commitment to equality, piqued interest and stimulated activism on the part of an increasing number of women's groups. The programs which became familiar to more and more women were not adequately serving the needs of their clientele. Was it lack of support by the president, poor management, insufficent funds, or enforcement authority? Experience with complaint procedures taught some practical lessons about all four factors.

Presidential Support

There was no effort on the part of the president to give strong and continuous support to antidiscrimination programs during his first administration. He failed to follow the specific recommendations of his task force on administrative matters. His appointments of women to high level policy positions lagged behind those of his predecessor, and no attempt was made to improve on this aspect of the recommendations until the spring of 1971. Appointments are still somewhere between 1 and 2 percent of the total. Inaccurate or camouflaged figures have been presented about them on several occasions by high officials. The president did nothing, publicly and, so far as could be determined, privately, to correct the sluggish performance of the major programs. He opposed legislation which would have improved their output. His single move, in the direction of national policy on the status of women, was to request that the Civil Rights Commission be granted authority to include sex discrimination within its jurisdiction.

The functions and scope of each of the programs have been contrasted with their ability to satisfy the demand that was made for their output in the course of the first Nixon administration, and been found wanting.

Women's Bureau

The one agency related to equality for women without enforcement functions, the Women's Bureau, has taken a limited view of its goals in terms of its legislative mandate. Its initial concentration on lobbying for state laws that would "protect" women by providing different working conditions for them than provided for men, which lasted for almost forty years, prevented it from widening its functions to include other aspects of concern to working women. Under Elizabeth Koontz's direction, some additional subjects were undertaken for research and services, but because the Bureau's budget has remained static for more than two decades, few functions were added that might have served the needs of increasing numbers of working women. The publicity it has given working conditions has helped to focus attention on discriminatory practices and their effects. Limited resources and deliberate efforts to lower its prestige and deplete its functions within the Labor Department have restricted its output to the dissemination of statistics of interest to working women, holding conferences and pilot projects on a number of subjects, including vocational training, and child care.

Equal Pay Act–Labor Department

Only one of the remaining programs, all of which are designed to enforce equal opportunity in private and public employment, is solely concerned with sex discrimination. It had long had the support of women's groups, both those which opposed and those which supported the ERA. Administration of the act, which enables complainants to conceal their identity, and which has a reputation for prompt and effective processing of cases, is generally regarded as effective. After eight years of handling a number of complaints (only 5 percent had to be taken to court), it was obvious that the continued difference between median wages paid to men and women was the result of discriminatory patterns, particularly the segregation of jobs which denied women employment opportunities.

The Federal Women's Program

Created by an executive order signed by President Johnson, and a by-product of the civil rights movement of the sixties rather than the women's movement, this program received an initial boost from President Nixon soon after he took office in 1969. As the program which depended on the Civil Service Commission to process complaints from aggrieved federal employees and to supervise an EEO program in every agency and department, it had, however, little impact on federal employment patterns during the first Nixon administration. Its administration has been severely criticized by a number of women in and outside the government for failing to enforce guidelines for firm programs, and for a grievance procedure which has rarely promoted aggrieved employees and does nothing to encourage speedy or consistent handling of complaints.

Contract Compliance—Labor Department

The lengthy delay in issuing guidelines for contract companies to follow in their efforts to abide by the contract compliance EO made it difficult to estimate the effectiveness of this phase of national policy on the status of women. Despite the request of the President's Task Force on Women's Rights and the increasing demand from women's groups that the EO be used more effectively to fight sex discrimination, "Revised Order No. 4," issued after it was decided that the original Order No. 4 establishing guidelines referred to every kind of discrimination mentioned in the EO except sex, was delayed until the middle of the last year of the first Nixon administration. The guidelines left many questions unanswered as legal cases multiplied. The only sanction against offenders, (i.e., withdrawal of government contracts) cannot be effective when the government is dealing with a "sole source" (e.g., large telephone companies and the like). While the contract compliance program may offer possibilities for the future, experience so far has been too limited, and the department's implementation too fragmentary, for final judgment.

Contract Compliance—HEW

Government officials admit that no effort was made to enforce the contract compliance program among 2,500 colleges and universities, so far as sex discrimination was concerned, until mid-way into the first Nixon administration. Even after WEAL had filed hundreds of charges, enforcement was sporadic and compliance reviews often too late to correct admittedly discriminatory situations. College and university officials and members of women's organizations complained frequently and forcefully about HEW Office for Civil Rights procedures. And, as in other contract compliance efforts, failure to make and implement policy decisions prevented speedy enforcement of the EO. Statistics continued to show that women faculty members were less favored from the standpoint of pay and promotion than men. Guidelines were finally issued during the summer of 1972, but a too-small staff and much larger responsibilities with passage of the Education Amendments of 1972 did not seem to argue for a speedy resolution for the backlog of complaints that OCR had experienced since 1971.

EEOC

The commission was created by Title VII of the Civil Rights Act of 1964 to implement prohibition of sex discrimination in private employment. A wide variety of employment practices came under the act, but jurisdiction was limited to firms with 25 or more employees, and there were other restrictions. Women's groups have been relatively satisfied with EEOC guidelines and court interpretations of them, but they have been dissatisfied with the slowness in handling complaints (EEOC had a backlog of more than 50,000 cases during 1972). Differentiation in jobs which can be restricted to males or females has been severely restricted—so much so that the only legitimate distinction that can be made by an employer occurs when "authenticity" or "genuineness" is involved. Contributing to the backlog of complaints was an inadequate budget and lack of enforcement power. Until mid-1972 EEOC could only investigate and conciliate complaints. Complainants had to seek enforcement of the law in court by themselves. The Department of Justice, which had the power to file suit, did so only once on behalf of a woman who had charged sex discrimination against an employer. Changes made by Congress in 1972 promised improvement, but experts believed it would come slowly.

3

The Congress Responds to the Women's Movement

More legislation of consequence to the cause of equal rights for women was passed in the 92nd Congress than had been enacted in all previous Congresses combined. Not everything that had been lobbied for by women's groups was passed. Congressional failures to add cease and desist power to the Equal Employment Opportunity Commission, and to extend equal pay and minimum wage benefits to millions of women workers at the bottom of the pay scale were particularly disappointing to feminist groups. But, lobbying by a coalition of new militant, and older, more established, groups had proved effective in passing the ERA, gaining some added power for the EEOC, the extension of Equal Pay Act provisions to women in executive, professional, and administrative positions and the prohibition of discrimination in higher education.

The recommendations of the Nixon Task Force on Women's Rights and Responsibilities had found favor with dozens of national women's groups, and even though an omnibus bill enacting its proposals did not get beyond the hearing stage, several of its recommendations were passed in the 92nd Congress. A coalition to pass the ERA (Women United), brought together representatives of both major political parties, the Federation of Business and Professional Women's Clubs, the newly formed (1971) National Women's Political Caucus, and several others to lobby for its passage. Loosely associated, initially, in the move to urge passage of the Amendment, many of the groups maintained a network of communications to coordinate lobbying on the Hill and in Congressional Districts for several other measures. The 1972 primary campaigns, with their emphasis upon more women on delegate slates, helped to mobilize women for Congressional lobbying, as well as presidential nominating activities. (For an analysis of the constituency of the women's groups and their mode of operation see Chapter 4.)

Many factors played a part in the increased attention Congress paid to an issue which had failed to claim its interest for such a long period of time. Most of the legislation sponsored by women's groups also had the support of large blocs of other lobbyists: organized labor, civil rights organizations, social welfare advocates, among others, and the Democratic leadership of both Houses. The Equal Rights Amendment, opposed by the AFL–CIO, had, as the result of intense lobbying by women's groups, gained a momentum of its own by the end of the 91st Congress. It passed the House in the second session by a large margin, but hit a snag in the Senate when it came up during the campaigning absence of senators who might have supported it. Opposition to the ERA later appeared during its consideration for ratification.

The justice of complaints about discrimination, as they were reviewed by individual legal experts and public advisory groups on the national, state and local levels, found a sympathetic audience. Increasing numbers of women in the work force, interacting with militant feminist groups in communities throughout the United States, made dodging the issue potentially dangerous for many members of the Congress.

The following legislation[1] affecting legal and economic discrimination against women was passed by the 92nd Congress:

The Equal Employment Opportunity Commission received increased enforcement power, and its jurisdiction was increased to cover more working women.

Sex discrimination was prohibited in all federally aided education programs, with exemptions granted only to admission standards in private undergraduate colleges and universities, military academies, religious training schools, and elementary and secondary schools, with the exception of vocational training schools. In this same legislation, provisions of the Equal Pay Act, ensuring equal pay for comparable work, were extended to administrative, professional and executive women employees.

Health profession training grantees, primarily medical and nursing schools, were forbidden to discriminate on the basis of sex.

The Civil Rights Commission, an independent group charged with objective reviews of national policy in the area of minority discrimination, was given jurisdiction over sex discrimination policy.

Parents with incomes of up to $18,000 a year were permitted to deduct up to $400 a month in child-care costs.

Federal employee benefits, cost-of-living allowances in foreign areas, and regulations concerning the marital status of federal employees were equalized for females.

Widows and widowers were to receive benefits under Social Security equal to 100 percent of the amount the deceased husband or wife would receive if still living.

Legislation favored by most organized women's lobbying groups, which did not pass, included child-care legislation (increases were made in the amount of federal funds to be provided for such care, but major legislation, which would have provided a full educational and nutritional program, was vetoed by the president); extension of the minimum wage and equal pay guarantees to millions of women workers; granting of full "cease and desist" power to the Equal Employment Opportunity Commission and, thus, speed-up of the tens of thousands of backlogged sex and minority complaints by the end of 1972; improvement in the Social Security and private pension systems, the inadequacies of which hit women harder because they lived longer and qualified, in most instances, for smaller amounts than men; correction of discriminatory features of banking practices which denied credit to millions of women despite the soundness of their financial background, and other matters related to unfair treatment of women in custom and the law.

The major legislation, which had been considered by the Congress and had the support of a number of groups, had factors in common which help to explain its treatment in the Congress and forecast the future course of legislation on the status of women. All of the legislation, as its supporters in and out of Congress frequently pointed out, was related to the fulfillment of national goals, which had the support of far more than militant women's groups. They were endorsed by older organizations, some of them concerned with the status of women in the professions, of women in business, a few auxiliaries of male organizations, and some traditionally involved in voluntarism in a variety of fields, from consumerism to child care. They were also by-products of issues which claimed the attention of organizations with large constituencies with no particular interest in advancing the cause of women's rights.

Political leaders ready to go on record opposed to equal legal and economic rights for women were a dwindling group. On the other hand, as the issue gained popularity, legislators willing to assume leadership roles in guiding legislation through Congress increased in number. Major legislation related to equality for women which was considered by the 92nd Congress deserves closer attention than can be given within these pages. In terms of our model of the decision-making process, however, salient factors in their legislative histories emerge from even a brief review. Major factors in the legislation which had importance for future legislation are worthy of analysis.

Equal Rights Amendment

The Equal Rights Amendment promised "instant equality" for women—an end to all laws and official practices which discriminated on the basis of sex. Foes of the amendment invariably cited the loss of legislation protecting women as the reason for their opposition. State after state, however, had by the early seventies amended protective labor laws, either by extending them to men when they involved an improvement in safety or health factors, or by outlawing them when they conflicted with national equal opportunity legislation (primarily Title VII of the Civil Rights Act of 1964). Opposition to the ERA diminished as an increasing number of federal and state laws mandated legal equality for women.

Old arguments based on the need for limiting hours of work for women, as well as fears (labelled groundless by almost, if not all, of the legal authorities researching the field) that the amendment would upset custody and alimony settlements favorable to women, came into play during ratification votes by several state legislatures in 1972 and 1973. Opposition forces included women who had supported the Goldwater candidacy in 1964, and were funded by business and industrial interests who feared the loss of a supply of cheaper labor with the end of legal discrimination.

Many women's organizations were puzzled by the active role the AFL-CIO played in attempting to defeat ratification of the ERA. Several major affiliated labor organizations supported the amendment, but a letter sent out by Andrew Biemiller in February, 1973 (addressed to the heads of AFL-CIO Councils as "Dear Sir and Brother"), reminded its membership of the passage of a resolution opposing ratification in November 1971 at their Ninth Constitutional Convention, and urged action to defeat the measure in the states which still had not ratified.[2] Tentative alliances formed by women's groups and labor in the support of the minimum wage and child care had failed to pave the way toward mutual understanding of this issue. The AFL-CIO and member unions were almost totally male-dominated. Whether they feared erosion of power as a result of the effect of the ERA on their own discriminatory practices, preferring to play the "protective" role their advocacy of special labor legislation for women suggested, or whether their opposition was the result of a failure to understand the dynamic implications of the steadily increasing number of women in the work force had to be a matter of conjecture.[3] It should be noted that many of the cases brought by women blue- and white-collar workers, under EEOC regulations, were directed at unions and, in several instances, courts had found collusion between unions and management in efforts to keep women segregated in lower paying jobs.

Despite opposition from organized labor, the ERA had received wide support when it passed the House of Representatives in 1970. Congressman Emanuel Celler's strategy of bottling up the amendment in the Judiciary Committee had yielded to a counter-parliamentary move by Congresswomen Martha Griffiths (D., Mich.). Celler, in the course of debate on the amendment, asked if it were "not passing strange that women have had the vote for over half a century and have used it not to elect women but to elect men?"[4] Celler got an answer to his question when a woman defeated him in a primary contest in his district the following year. (Elizabeth Holtzman was elected to Congress from Celler's former stronghold in November, 1972.) An amendment designed to "cripple" the ERA, by qualifying its application to all women, was defeated in the House in 1971 by a vote of 265 to 87; the amendment itself passed on October 12, 1971 by a vote of 354 to 23.

In the Senate, Senator Sam J. Ervin (D., N.C.) declared himself responsible for the mobilization of a dwindling opposition force. Birch Bayh (D., Ind.) and Marlow Cook (R., Ky.) led the move to pass ERA after its successful vote in the House. The largest number of votes mustered for an opposition amendment that might have tabled ERA, as it had in the previous Congress, was seventeen. After days of opposition, debate led by Ervin who relied on arguments that ERA would insure the drafting of women for combat duty (the fact that no constitutional amendment was needed to give Congress the power to draft women if it so chose, since it already had it, repeatedly escaped the attention of Ervin and others who used the argument) and that it would mean the end of privacy in the toilet, the amendment passed with 84 in favor and only 8 opposed. Additional major legislation affecting equality for women included the Education Amendments of 1972, and stronger enforcement powers for the Equal Employment Opportunity Commission. The latter bill received support from women's groups and a coalition of liberal interest groups and Congressmen, and was opposed by a Republication-Southern Democratic coalition and the White House. Efforts to strengthen enforcement against discrimination in employment has had a lengthy history. The addition of women's groups and their constituencies was an important element in the passage of such legislation in the 92nd Congress.

Equal Employment Opportunities Act

Whether cease and desist power should be part of the federal enforcement effort to combat discrimination had been an issue when the bill was first considered by Congress. When the Civil Rights Act of 1964 was reported in the House it had included authority to issue such orders to companies found to be following employment practices in violation of the act. While under consideration on the House floor, however, the enforcement power was reduced to authority to issue injunctions against an employers found to be in violation. In the Senate version of the bill, this power was further reduced. President Lyndon B. Johnson repeatedly asked Congress to add cease and desist authority to the commission created by the Civil Rights Act of 1964. The House approved it in 1966, but the Senate failed to act; in 1968, when a Senate Committee reported a bill containing cease and desist power, the late Senator Everett M. Dirksen (R., Ill.) announced his intention to lead a filibuster against it and the bill was again defeated. Finally, in the 91st Congress the Senate passed a bill giving the EEOC cease and desist power after rejecting a Nixon-sponsored amendment to substitute a weaker form of enforcement. This bill was lost in the House, however, when the Rules Committee did not report it.

The bill, which appeared ready for more affirmative action in the 92nd Congress, included other features besides the granting of cease and desist power to the EEOC.[5] It would have expanded coverage of minority and sex discrimination provisions to employers and unions with eight or more employees or members, to employees of state and local governments, to employees of the federal government, and to employees of educational institutions (including teachers). The "pattern or practice" jurisdiction by which the government can itself take class suits involving large groups of employees to court, originally given to the Justice Department by the 1964 Act, was transferred to the EEOC. When this bill was reported by the House Committee on Education and Labor in the late summer of 1971, the White House was ready with an alternative bill, introduced by Congressman John Erlenborn (R., Ill.), which was considerably weaker. Perhaps its greatest weakening provision was one which would have established Title VII of the

Civil Rights Act of 1964 as the only remedy for unlawful employment practices, superseding all other Civil Rights Acts, the Equal Pay Act, and other legislation. Class actions were prohibited, and only the attorney general was permitted to intervene in private actions. Coverage of employers and unions would have remained the same. This bill was accepted as a substitute for the liberal committee version, to the surprise of many supporters of the latter measure, by a vote of 202 to 197.

In the Senate, a version very similar to the original House Committee bill was reported out of the Labor Committee late in October, 1971. Its sponsor, Senator Harrison Williams (D., N.J.), and Senate Leader Mike Mansfield (D., Mont.) responding to the threat of a filibuster from Republican-Southern Democratic sources, under the leadership of Peter Dominick (R., Colo.), postponed action until the second session of Congress. Attorneys Thomas J. Hart and George Sape, in an article detailing the legislative history of the Equal Employment Opportunities Act, report that the real issue was the type of enforcement the Congress would select—cease and desist or the milder kind of enforcement the White House preferred. Conservative Southern opposition to any kind of added enforcement power was not sufficiently strong to defeat the bill. When it reached the floor, finally, in January 1972 the tactic "was not to declare a filibuster but to introduce numerous amendments to each portion of the bill that (opponents) found objectionable, and then force a vote on each amendment."[6]

Votes on various controversial features of the bill seesawed back and forth, the decisions sometimes dependent on calling back liberal Democratic senators campaigning in the presidential primaries. A total of 87 amendments were offered to S 2515, with Senators James B. Allen (D., Ala.) and Ervin contributing the lion's share. As debate on amendments dragged on, Senator Jacob Javits (R., N.Y.) and Williams brought matters to a head with a cloture vote, which failed. Debate would end, the conservative coalition leaders indicated, only when cease and desist was eliminated. A Dominick amendment removing the strong enforcement power from the bill was permitted to carry after Senator Jacob Javits, speaking on the floor of the Senate, admitted that supporters of the Williams bill in its stronger form did not have enough votes for cloture. When Senator Ervin declared that he could not go along with ending debate because his opposition to the bill went beyond his negative feelings about cease and desist authority, enough Republicans joined the liberal coalition to vote cloture by a vote of 73 to 21. Thus, on February 22, 1972, the long wrangle over the discrimination measure ended, with the tenth vote to end debate in the Senate since the cloture rule was adopted in 1917. The bill itself passed later the same day by a vote of 73 to 16. Only a few substantive issues remained for the conference committee. Unquestionably, the bill strengthened the federal enforcement arm against sex and minority discrimination in employment. Its more positive features included:

Millions more workers were covered, including state and local employees, those in establishments with 14 or more employees, unions with 14 or more members, and employees of educational institutions.

Federal employees were now covered by statute, rather than executive order, and could go to court if they were not satisfied with the way the Civil Service Commission was handling their complaint.

The Equal Employment Opportunity Commission gained the power to file suit in court to gain compliance; and, after a two-year period in which it shared authority to bring pattern or practice suit with the Department of Justice, EEOC could have sole authority to bring such action.[7]

Sape and Hart, both of whom have had extensive experience with EEOC legislation, were optimistic about the long-run possibilities the measure offers. They warned that its enforcement effort was "fated to begin slowly . . . ."

The EEOC . . . has traditionally been hampered by inadequate funding and a shortage of staff with which to meet the rising number of complaints of employment discrimination. These problems, compounded by six years of operation under the original, inadequate powers contained in Title VII, have resulted in administrative problems and an ever-increasing backlog of pending charges which will further slow the agency's ability to undertake effectively the new responsibilities which it has been granted.[8]

By spring of 1973, the EEOC's backlog of complaints was approaching 70,000, some 30 percent of which concerned sex discrimination. EEOC also had the task of developing new guidelines as the result of the 1972 legislation. It was very likely that a number of the cases "initiated during the next few years will be brought primarily to resolve procedural questions. This," the authors acknowledged, "will further delay Commission operations and will divert Commission resources from that litigation which is aimed at obtaining quick and effective remedies for aggrieved claimants." Yet many experts familiar with employment discrimination legislation and administration believed that the new law had opened up the possibilities for an all-out attack on employment discrimination. At least, in the view of many, it dispelled any doubts as to the seriousness of federal intent in correcting such discrimination.[9]

Title IX of the Education Amendments of 1972

Title IX of the Education Amendments of 1972, passed by the 92nd Congress as a means of correcting sex discrimination at the college and university level, had a complex legislative history. Introduced during the 91st Congress by Representative Green as a section of an Omnibus Education Bill, it had broad coverage—it was to amend the Civil Rights Act so as to prohibit discrimination on the basis of sex, and to eliminate the exemption in Title VII of the Act which left employees of educational institutions, including teachers, without redress against this kind of discrimination. It also would have authorized the Civil Rights Commission to study discrimination against women and would have removed the exemption of executive, administrative, and professional employees from the equal pay for equal work provisions of the Fair Labor Standards Act. Hearings in June 1970 were the first held by Congress, Representative Green has pointed out, to deal exclusively with sex discrimination in employment in education.[10] Representatives of the movement had an opportunity to testify on a number of different aspects of discrimination against working women, including those employed at universities who had found little protection granted to them by the chief agency of the federal government functioning in the area—the Office for Civil Rights of HEW.

The bill, on which hearings had been held too late for action in the 91st Congress, was reintroduced in the 92nd. Congressman Erlenborn, who functioned on the Education subcommittee as a representative of the administration as well as the Republican minority in Congress, claimed that abolishing sex discrimination in private undergraduate colleges would be burdensome for certain institutions. A compromise was reached and a bill passed by the House in November, 1971, which forbade sex discrimination in all federally aided school programs but as a result of the opposition efforts, exempted admissions to all undergraduate institutions, religious institutions where religious beliefs conflicted with the purposes of the Act. Institutions not exempted whose enrollments had been confined to one sex were given seven years to complete the process of integration.[11]

The sex discrimination amendment had passed by a close vote (194 to 189), but the attention of the Congress was directed primarily toward other features of the Omnibus Education Bill. In the House it had been combined with an Emergency School Aid Bill, and amendments added to it which would have restricted the use of funds in the busing of public school children for the purpose of racial integration. There are some who believe that, if it had not been for the addition of the antibusing amendments and the desire of many representatives to get on an antiintegration bandwagon, the bill with its sex discrimination features might not have passed. In the Senate, they had been left out of the bill when it was first reported, and efforts by Senator Bayh to add them had been ruled nongermane by the Senate. The Senate bill came up for reconsideration in February, and Bayh reintroduced the sex discrimination amendment. Debate in the Senate centered on other features of the bill, however; particularly, the antibusing amendments, with the Senate finally taking action on a compromise amendment which was less stringent than the House version. The conference committee eventually adopted the mildest of the three provisions which had been included in its bill.

The education act which finally passed as a combined emergency school aid-aid to higher education measure authorized $19 billion in aid for postsecondary education through fiscal 1975. Its sex discrimination title was broad in coverage: "No person in the United States shall, on the basis of sex, be excluded from participation in, be denied the benefits of, or be subjected to discrimination under any education program or activity receiving federal financial assistance." Exemptions applied only to equal admissions policies. Students once admitted to a course of study must not be subjected to discrimination. Discrimination in admission was prohibited in vocational schools, including high schools, institutions of professional and graduate higher education, and public undergraduate coeducational institutions.[12]

Sex discrimination in higher education was one of the issues suggested as a subject for investigation by the Nixon Task Force on Women's Rights and Responsibilities. While some women in the Nixon administration gave their endorsement to the Green bill, officially the White House opposed most of its sex discrimination measures, including extension of the Equal Pay Act[13] to more women employees and nondiscriminatory admission policies for private colleges and universities. Activist groups, particularly the Women's Equity Action League, led the way toward emphasis upon discrimination on college campuses, as prejudice hindered qualified women in pursuit of academic and administrative appointments, and in the training of women for careers in fields such as medicine, law, and engineering, from which they had been virtually excluded for generations. Debate on the measure was carried on quietly in Congress, primarily because of the introduction of the highly charged antibusing amendments. Few private colleges (only Amherst among Ivy League schools) were not admitting women. Those that had opened their doors to women promised to provide thousands of women with educations which previously had been denied to them.

Major Legislation That Failed

Very close votes on legislation concerning various aspects of sex discrimination issues, particularly the extension of minimum wage and equal pay coverage to millions of women workers, in the 92nd Congress, resulted from White House and conservative congressional opposition, an alliance operating in other issue areas. While child-care legislation only indirectly concerns sex discrimination, it was strongly supported by many women's rights groups and countless volunteer and social welfare organizations with large numbers of women members. These and other defeats registered for the movement in 1971-72 were important items on the agenda of women's organizations for the future.

Minimum Wage

The minimum wage for working men and women was $1.60 an hour when the Congress went into action on proposed increases of both the wage itself and the number of workers covered by it in 1971. As the Senate Committee Report[14] on the bill pointed out, $1.60 an hour yielded the head of a family of four only $3,200, almost $800 less than the poverty level. Extension of minimum wage coverage in the early seventies would be of greater significance to women and blacks than to white men, primarily because of the kinds of occupation held by them, which were paid at or below the minimum. The Senate bill amending the Fair Labor Standards Act as reported, would have particularly affected working women in several ways:

Extended coverage to 8.4 million additional workers, including household workers; and to federal, state and local government employees, and to retail workers, of whom more than half were women;

Provided a four-step increase for agricultural workers (of whom 70 percent are women), to an hourly wage of $1.60 (from $1.30) when enacted, increasing to $1.80 in 1973 and $2 in 1974;

Repealed or modified minimum wage and/or overtime exemptions for motion-picture theater employees, tobacco workers, agricultural processing, sea food processing and local transit workers;

Extended the coverage of nondiscrimination because of age to federal, state, and local government employees (unemployed women over 50 outnumber men by several percentage points);

All workers previously covered, who had received coverage before passage of the 1966 amendments (retail, service workers in firms with gross annual sales in excess of $1 million; most private firms engaged primarily in interstate commerce, or the production of goods for interstate commerce) were to receive a minimum wage of $2 per hour upon enactment and $2.20 the following year. Women retail and service workers had increased in number more than any other group from 1960 to 1970;

Those workers covered since 1966 (all businesses with gross annual sales of $250,000 or more) were to receive a three-step increase to $1.80 upon enactment, $2 in 1973 and $2.20 in 1975;

The basic work week (after which overtime must be paid) was reduced for nursing homes and bowling establishments;

Exemption was lifted from hotel, motel, and restaurant employees, cotton-ginning, sugar-processing workers, catering and food service employees. Service workers and operatives in these jobs include a substantial number of women.

The arguments made on behalf of its bill, by those in the majority on the committee (headed by Sen. Harrison Williams), cited the inadequacy of the present wage, the fact that losses due to inflation needed to be made up, stimulation of the economy which would result from higher wages, and reduction of welfare rolls by the increase in wages for millions of borderline poverty families. Republicans on the committee, representing the views of the White House, countered with arguments stressing that the bill would make job opportunities more difficult, increase inflation, and hurt farmers and small businessmen.

The defeat of the bill was the product of concerted lobbying by business groups, and the steady and active hand of Republicans in Congress, with generous support from the White House staff. The bill reported by the committee was similar to the more liberal measure reported by the Senate committee, with an exception worthy of note: employment of students at a wage rate equal to 85 percent of the minimum wage applicable to the occupation, or $1.60 an hour, whichever was higher. This provision particularly offended labor.

Republicans, aided by a strong grassroots campaign by Chambers of Commerce throughout the United States, successfully employed a number of techniques to set aside the Democrat-supported measure and replace it with a weaker version. The Rules Committee cooperated by delaying the legislation for a period of six months, finally sending the bill to the floor on May 9, 1972, under an "open rule." This was a gesture of defiance to the House leadership, since most bills are sent to the floor with a rule limiting debate and amendments. The Chairman of the Rules Committee, William M. Colmer (D., Miss.) made his opposition to the bill clear during hearings before the Rules Committee, thus foreshadowing the fully developed opposition to come from the southern Democratic-Republican coalition mobilized to defeat it or to substitute a bill with a lower minimum wage and no extension of coverage. The vote adopting amendments suggested by Congressman Erlenborn was 217 to 191. Aside from narrowing the scope of the bill, the wage increase for nonfarm workers was to be $1.80 an hour in 1972 and $2 an hour in 1973. In a key vote of 216 to 187, this part of the bill was further weakened by an amendment offered by Representative John B. Anderson (R., Ill.) which lengthened the wage boost two steps, one 60 days after enactment, and the second a year later.

Two additional provisions of the Republican substitute bill should be noted, both strongly opposed by organized labor. The import restrictions were removed, and the employment of youth under the age of 18, or students under the age of 21 at 80 percent of the appropriate minimum wage for the position, or $1.60 an hour (whichever was greater), permitted. Future consideration of the minimum wage bill hinged on the defeat of the coalition which overcame the move to send the Senate and the House versions of the bill to conference. Southern Democrats (47), 148 Republicans and 3 northern Democrats united to defeat a motion by the chairman of the House Education and Labor Committee to request a conference, a move which succeeded in ending chances for an increase in the minimum wage in the 92nd Congress.

Very early in the following Congress, liberal Democratic forces made clear their intention to renew the fight for the minimum wage. As allies, organized labor had all of the major feminist organizations and several hundred smaller national and local organizations. Plans were under way for an alliance which could have meaning for much legislation beyond minimum wage. The Senate bill, more liberal than the House version, would have increased the minimum wage to $2 per hour immediately and raised it to $2.20 an hour one year later for all those who had been covered by the FLSA prior to 1966. A measure resembling the Senate version was passed by Congress in July, 1973, and, at this writing, awaited the President's signature.

Child Care

Child care needs are of particular concern to working women, some 40 percent of whom have children under the age of 14. Day care facilities are inadequate for most of these women, because private day care is too expensive and subsidized day care not available except for the very poor. Legislation was introduced in the 92nd Congress, which attempted to satisfy demand for improved child care facilities in two ways—by providing spaces for children in adequate numbers, and by mandating federal standards for day care beyond simple custodial care, to include a wide range of educational, cultural and nutritional services. The Child Development bill authorized $2.1 billion for the establishment of comprehensive child development programs, with services provided on a sliding pay scale for middle- and low-income families. It had the support of 26 national public interest groups, including trade unions, the U. S. Catholic Conference, and the League of Women Voters. The bill was the subject of compromise by both Houses as Senate leaders Walter F. Mondale (D., Minn.) and Javits and House proponents John Brademas (D., Ind.) and Ogden Reid (D., N.Y.), struggled to provide a bill that would fulfill the goals of its supporters and survive a threatened presidential veto. [15]

Part of legislation extending the life of the Office of Economic Opportunity, the provisions were subjected to intense discussion by a conference committee for a period of more than a month in the fall of 1971. Republican conferees worked closely with Secretary Richardson and believed they had the president's approval for the compromise provisions that were developed. The bill that emerged from conference was described by economist Alice Rivlin as "not just a babysitting operation"; it emphasized the "well-being of children and the comprehensive services they need for full development, whether their mothers work or not." Designed to aid families at all income levels, its "prime sponsor" mechanism and parent councils specifically bypassed state welfare bureaucracies and gave program clientele a say in its operation.

Its major provisions included, under Title V, Child Development Programs; $2 billion was authorized for these programs in fiscal 1973, including $500,000 for Headstart programs.

Funds were to be allocated among the states according to a formula, administered directly at the local level. (Communities of 5,000 or more could apply to be prime sponsors and receive funds directly from the federal government.) In the course of debate in the conference committee, in deference to administration wishes, somewhat more control over funds was given to the states.

Families of four with incomes of less than $4,320 were to receive child care services free; for those with higher incomes, fees were payable on a sliding scale. (Those with incomes of $6,960 a year, for example, would pay $317 a year.) [16]

The bill's supporters, including congressmen who thought they had guided it successfully past the danger of administration disapproval, were stunned when the president vetoed the measure in December, 1971. The veto message cited the Child Development program as "the most deeply flawed provision" of the entire OEO extension bill. In the light of later history it should be noted that the bill included the requirement that legislative approval be required for dismantling any OEO program. The president's opposition to the philosophy of child care, which so many national organizations had embraced, was made very clear. He did not believe in the need for day care as proposed in the bill, indicating that his welfare proposals (i.e., H.R. 1, which included requirements that women with small children leave their children in centers and go to work) were sufficient. The Child Development Bill was a "long leap into the dark" and "the most radical piece of legislation to emerge from the 92nd Congress." He asked for lengthy national debate on the issue which he believed would cost too much, moved in the opposite direction from welfare reform, would diminish parental authority, create a new army of bureaucrats and relegate the states to an insignificant role. Finally, the bill would "commit the vast moral authority of the National Government to the side of communal approaches to child rearing over against the family centered approach."[17] The latter comment provoked Theodore Taylor of the Day Care and Child Developmental Council, of which the president's wife had been honorary chairman, to ask if public schools were "communal approaches" . . . or "choirs and orchestras . . . ?"

A senate attempt to override the president's veto failed. The efforts of the sponsors of the original bill to develop new legislation which might escape another veto died with the end of the second session.

Developing Issues—Other Legislation

Other legislation considered in the 92nd Congress reflected the development of a number of issues in areas of particular interest to women: an equalization of income tax deductions, improved pension plans for women retiring under private and/or Social Security benefits, prohibition of discrimination in the granting of credit, improved maternity benefits in employment insurance plans, continuation and improvement of maternity and infant care programs, aid to research in contraception as well as improved birth control aid available to all, antidiscrimination measures added to revenue sharing bills, and additional equalization of employment benefits in the public and private sector. Legislation that passed the 92nd Congress included:

The Social Security Act amendments, which increased taxes as well as benefits, corrected certain inequities in the distribution of the latter. Married couples may now obtain a percentage of old-age benefits based on their combined earnings, and widows or widowers' benefits are to equal 100 percent of the amount the decreased husband or wife would receive if still living. The requirement that divorced women show that they were dependent on their husbands for their support in order to receive benefits was removed. Under Medicare-Medicaid provisions, 90 percent of federal funding for the costs of family planning services was authorized, and states required to make such services available on a voluntary and confidential basis to any present, former, or likely welfare recipient of childbearing age who asks for them.

Income-tax deductions for child-care payments survived in the 92nd Congress tax revenue bill, although several other personal deductions had been dropped. The amendment to the bill, which provided deductions of up to $400 a month for day care for children under the age of 15, was sponsored by Finance Committee Chairman Russell Long (D., La.). An amendment, which would have made deductions available to families with lower incomes who use standard deductions rather than itemized, was offered by Senator John V. Tunney (D., Ca.) on the floor and passed, although it was later removed by the conferees before final passage. As it was passed, the deduction is available if a parent works at least six hours a day or 30 hours a week, and the combined income of husband and wife does not exceed $18,000 a year. As much as $400 may be deducted for care for one or more children. Deductions at increasingly lower rates may be taken for incomes as high as $27,600 a year. The measure has been criticized on two counts—because it discriminated against families with lower incomes and because it is the only itemized deduction with an income level limit.

The Civil Rights Commission's jurisdiction was enlarged to include review of national policy on sex discrimination. The commission had been established in 1957 to protect the rights of minorities. Its resources had gone to "hearings, investigations and reports . . . (documenting) the need for many of the civil rights laws and (participating) in the effort to enactment." Until the 92nd Congress added sex discrimination to the act which authorized its existence for another five years, CRC had reviewed programs which included women's rights issues but not dealt specifically with the subject. The law authorized increased funding (5.5 million for 1973 and 7 million a year for 1974–1978). Reporting the bill, the Senate Judiciary Committee said that it favored

the inclusion of sex discrimination as a logical expansion of the Commission's jurisdiction. . . .The Committee furthermore hopes . . . that particular attention be given to the special problems of minority women when the Commission turns its attention to the problem of sex discrimination in general.[18]

The Revenue-Sharing Act passed by the 92nd Congress contained antidiscrimination provisions designed to insure that national policy on the status of women and minorities would be carried out in the course of expenditures of funds at state and local levels. The law provides that noncompliance with antidiscrimination provisions must be corrected within "a reasonable length of time." Critics point out that noncompliance for most provisions requires corrective action within 60 days. For some kinds of noncompliance, the act provides for withholding of all funds until compliance has occurred. In the case of discrimination, only the funds of the program found in violation are to be cut off. There was also the danger that funds for programs that discriminate might be siphoned off from other programs which are not discriminatory, and revenue-sharing monies used for these programs, while the local government units that discriminated (e.g., fire departments against Blacks) could continue as before.

Amendments to Titles VII and VIII of the Public Health Act passed in 1972 prohibited discrimination in health training institutions funded by the act. The new legislation promised to guarantee more women financial backing for medical schools, while men who wanted to enter predominantly female training courses had to be admitted. The bill covered all private and public institutions, including some which had previously been exempted. Funds authorized included loans to students, with cancellation provisions of up to 30 percent for the first two years of service in areas with critical health manpower shortages, and 25 percent for the third year of service; scholarship grants of up to $5,000 per year directly to medical students who agreed to practice in shortage areas, medical education initiative awards for practice in areas where there is a shortage of family doctors, and, also, to increase the admission of qualified individuals from minority and low-income groups.

Legislation which was considered, and failed, and which would still have a high priority among women's groups in the seventies included reform of the welfare system, so that women with small children would be protected in every state and not be subject to "workfare" (a slang word combining work and welfare) requirements; passage of provisions of the Women's Equality Act which had not been approved by Congress in 1971-72, and which included the prohibition of discrimination in public accommodations, forbidding discrimination in credit, provision of pensions for activity as head of household under the Social Security system, as well as special protection for the health of women under a national health insurance plan.

Women members of organizations could cite major achievements as the result of the activities of the 92nd Congress—as well as some major setbacks. The opportunity for lobbying and, in many instances, for successfully lobbying, was considerable during this Congress, and many organizations profited not only from the experience it provided but from alliances formed with other groups. Helpful relationships were established with congressional aides and, in some instances, with federal program staff members. There were a number of major issues unresolved that formed agenda items for the future as the final session came to a close. Inevitably, the growth in interest in the issue among policy makers and constituents alike was accompanied by an increase in the complexity of the issue itself. More bills meant greater diversion of interest and a need to maximize resources, which did not grow in proportion to the need for lobbying. All of the women's rights sub-issues were related to the general background of domestic policy. The state of the economy, the policies of a president who had won "49 to 1," the developing backlash among conservative groups opposing ERA and chauvinist trade union leaders, formed a challenging background to the further development of issues which most women's groups had found challenging enough in themselves.

4

The Women's Rights Lobby—Its Resources and Constituents

Agreement on political questions resulted in cooperative lobbying by a number of women's organizations from 1969 to 1972. But, as the first Nixon administration drew to a close, those who had worked hardest to understand the basics of policy on the status of women, and then to move it toward the national goal of full equality, faced an uncertain future. Ratification of the Equal Rights Amendment had met with unexpected opposition in several states. The president had for the most part merely given lip service to the goals of the movement; there was uncertainty as to whether he would do more or even less than that in his second administration. A resurgent conservative coalition in the Congress had defeated minimum wage legislation and successfully watered down other legislation designed to end sex and minority discrimination. Congressional effectiveness in advancing the status of women had improved over previous years, but the votes had been close. There was no assurance that additional legislation committing national resources to the goal of equal opportunity would be forthcoming.

Cohesiveness in pursuit of goals among women's groups had been impressive. Democratic women leaders strongly endorsed the goals of the Nixon Task Force on Women's Rights and Responsibilities and its recommendations. Older, established women's volunteer and career groups, began in the sixties to take an increasing interest in women's rights issues. Women's clubs, medical, scientific, educational, legal, and other organizations that had been formed to advance the career status of women began to be more sensitive to the general, pervasive nature of discrimination against women and to favor positive steps to end it. Groups formed in the late sixties, including caucuses within professional and occupational associations, and militant politically oriented organizations readily identified with a set of goals for the national effort to end sex discrimination. Only the radical Marxist groups (constituting a small fraction of all the politically oriented women's organizations), saw little point in supporting congressional and administration action in support of women's rights. To the right, most of the women opposing the Equal Rights Amendment, and who were identified with the labor movement did not openly challenge equal opportunity legislation, and a group of conservatives headed by Phyllis Schafly, who had lost out as leader of Republican women a few years before, never specifically opposed equal pay or opportunity for women in their literature. One of their arguments against the ERA, in fact, was that the passage of laws ending discrimination negated the need for the amendment.

It was apparent by the early seventies, however, that more than unanimity of purpose was needed if optimal national policy on the status of women was to be achieved. Two major problems appeared to face any and all organizations supporting equality for women—a need to widen participation in the political effort on the part of blue-collar and minority women, and to increase and maximize the necessary resources to support a massive lobbying effort. Cultural "lag" on the one hand, fear of change misidentified as *caused* by the women's movement, influenced the attitudes of large numbers of both men and women.

Despite the length of time goals of equality for women had been recognized in the national rhetoric, the women's rights issue was a relatively new item of national concern. Older issue areas have produced programs that have been in action for a couple of decades or longer. Interest groups have developed continuous supporting memberships, offices, and experienced staffs. At the same time, members of bureau and congressional subcommittee staffs also have acquired expertise over periods of time, and, dealing on a day-to-day basis with each other as well as with interest groups, developed relationships which make for ease (if not speed) and continuity in policy making.

In the late sixties, as the movement intensified, women's groups for the most part lacked experience as Hill or bureau lobbyists. Resources were slim in terms of expertise and money. At the same time, interest group inexperience was matched by lack of knowledge and lack of awareness of feminist goals on the part of both Hill and agency staffs. Staffs of representatives, with a deep interest in national policy on sex discrimination—Bella Azbug, Martha Griffiths, Patsy Mink, and Edith Green, among others—bore the burden of building up knowledge about women's rights issues in the Congress. Major components of an interest group constituency had formed, however, and data about its resources and structure needs to be analyzed, if the present and potential effectiveness of a "woman's rights lobby," united behind a variety of goals, is to be understood.

Clientele of Women's Rights Programs

Like federal programs in all domestic issue areas, those created in the sixties to carry out Congressional mandates on sex discrimination had a clientele of women who were in need of their services, or who sought help in the enforcement of government regulation against sex discrimination. All working women stood to gain from these programs. Only a few women, however, joined or actively participated in groups with goals related to influencing the output of these programs.

Women in the labor movement had made the Women's Bureau an object of their attention since its formation in 1920. Labor organizations, particularly the United Automobile Workers, took a particular interest in Bureau activities. Other national organizations which were concerned with working conditions for women included the National Council of Jewish Women, the National Council of Catholic Women, the National Consumers League, the General Federation of Women's Clubs, and the American Association of

University Women. The representatives of those who had followed government policy on women assembled by the President's Commission on the Status of Women in 1961, included leaders of some of these groups and many more. They refrained from pressuring for stricter enforcement power to federal programs, and chose to ask for greater social welfare programs for women and a continuation of protective legislation in the states. The Women's Bureau's constituency of interest groups, with limited goals of their own, naturally limited its demand for greater federal activity to what they believed in: equal pay for comparable work for women, with full, federally enforced equal opportunity programs in private employment, to be accomplished in easy stages.

The new militant spirit among groups, some decades old, and some very new (which became noticeable toward the end of the sixties), prompted a different outlook on national goals. These organizations covered an increasingly wider range of interests and occupations. Their militancy, numbers and goals were greater by far than those of the earlier women's rights constituency. Groups which supported a heavily intensified national effort to reach equality for women through passage and ratification of the Equal Rights Amendment *and* a full commitment of federal resources to end economic and legal sex discrimination may be divided into categories:[1]

1. There were three national, politically activist organizations of state and local units organized to influence national policy on the status of women and to encourage their local chapters to influence state and local policy.

   The National Organization for Women (NOW) was formed in 1966 under the leadership of Betty Friedan, author of *The Feminine Mystique,* and Kathryn Clarenbach, then head of the Wisconsin Commission on the Status of Women and others. Emphasizing the need for political action, task forces were set up to deal with "the problems of women in employment, education, religion, poverty, law, politics, and their image in the media." At NOW's convention in February 1973, lobbying on the state level (for the immediate goal of ratifying the ERA) and among Congressmen on a "one-to-one" basis, with a NOW-member assigned to each legislator for the purpose of lobbying organization goals was stressed by its 1973 president, Wilma Scott Heide, and legislation vice-president, Ann Scott. The meeting emphasized, particularly, the economic problems of women as they were reflected in cases before the EEOC, in establishing business firms, and in other ways. It has several hundred chapters and about 50,000 members.

   The Women's Equity Action League (WEAL) was organized in 1968 "to promote greater economic progress for women and to develop solutions to their economic, educational, and legal problems." Attracting, for the most part, a somewhat older, more established group than NOW, it is perhaps best known for its leadership in implementing the contract compliance executive order as it applied to sex discrimination. Attorney members, aid in many administrative and court cases as they apply to economic equality for women. WEAL also sponsors a Washington newsletter, which sums up legislation pending in the Congress and other items about national policy concerning the status of women for its members, who have now formed more than 30 state chapters. Heading the national organization in 1973 was Arvonne Fraser, formerly president of its Washington chapter.

The National Women's Political Caucus (NWPC) was formed in July 1971 to gain more political power for women, primarily by helping women candidates for public and party office, Liz Carpenter, Mrs. Lyndon B. Johnson's aide in the White House, Gloria Steinem, and others, have been responsible for its remarkable progress since. It also lobbies for federal action on the status of women, and, by 1973, had about 500 local units with a membership of about 50,000, including a scattered minority representation. It had a particularly stormy session at its 1973 convention when formal structuring of the organization was attempted for the first time. At that meeting, Frances Farenthold, a former Texas legislator and unsuccessful Democratic candidate for Governor of Texas, was elected national chairperson. National, politically oriented groups also included the National Woman's Party, established by suffragist Alice Paul in 1913, which, after passage of the Suffrage amendment, continued to function as a national group working "to improve the status of women." From 1923 on, it concentrated its efforts on the passage of the ERA. By the seventies it had chapters in every state and over 10,000 members. In its efforts to pass ERA, it was joined by two ad hoc coalition groups: Women United, which formed to help lobby the amendment through Congress, and, later, an ERA Ratification Council, with some twenty to thirty groups participating. Another umbrella group, calling itself The Clearing House on Women's Issues, attempted to bring together women's groups which had supported equal pay for women "for communication and common action on economic and educational issues as they affect women." Joint action, when "necessary" was promised, but only in the name of individual organizations supporting action on any particular issue.

2. Organizations of career women in professional, managerial, or entrepreneurial positions have, as a primary purpose, the promotion of women within such occupational categories, and, as one of a series of secondary goals, the advancement of the status of women in general. The Federation of Business and Professional Women's Clubs (BPW), founded in 1919, and composed of state federations and local clubs whose total membership is around 170,000 working women has as its chief goal the improvement of occupational status for its members. It supports the "Equal Rights Amendment to the Constitution as well as legislation in such areas as employment, social security, child care, education and taxes." Its former president, Virginia Allan, was chairperson of the Nixon Task Force on Women's Rights and Responsibilities, and later received a high level appointment in the State Department. The BPW was encouraged to begin a talent bank for policy

positions in the federal government, and maintained one for that purpose throughout the first Nixon administration. There were very few appointments from it, however.

National groups that had formed in the teens and twenties, and were still active, included some ten or fifteen other professional groups, among them the National Association of Women Lawyers, the American Medical Women's Association, the Association of American Women Dentists, the Association of Women in Architecture, Zonta International, the Intercollegiate Association of Women Students, the National Association of Bank Women, the National Association of College Women (for Negro women college graduates), the National Association for Women Deans, Administrators and Counselors, the National Council of Administrative Women in Education, the Society of Women Geographers, and the Women's National Press Club.

The League of Women Voters, an outgrowth of the National American Women Suffrage Association, was formed during the postwar period (1920). Its early interest in women's issues gradually diminished in favor of other national issues. By the early seventies, however, it had firmly endorsed the ERA and worked for its ratification. Only a few groups were as consistently active as the BPW and the National Association of Women Lawyers in the cause of women's rights. During the late sixties many of the older organizations became increasingly concerned with legal and economic equality for all women, and began to take steps to arouse their membership to the need for lobbying activity. A resurgent feminism in the late 1960s brought with it the creation of several professional women's organizations similar to those which developed during and immediately after the fight for suffrage. The major differences between the new groups and the older were twofold: first, the new organizations were much more numerous, covering professions and occupations that had never had women's units before, and, second, they were much more militant in their attitudes toward national policy on sex discrimination. Caucuses or groups were formed in every social or natural science subdivision, thirty to forty of them in the late sixties alone. An umbrella organization, calling itself the Federation of Organizations for Professional Women, was formed after more than forty groups convened in November of 1972 to discuss ways to increase their impact on advancing career status and national policy. Many of the groups, particularly in professions that were not lucrative for male or female members and where women were a small minority, found it difficult to maintain themselves as national organizations and felt compelled to maximize slender resources by combining functions with other groups.

3. One must also consider nonprofessional occupational groups. Some unions with large female memberships had promoted their own concept of optimal national policy (against ERA, for equal pay) over a long period of time. Their militancy—with the exception of a few, such as the UAW and the International Union of Electrical Workers—was

limited to support for protective labor legislation until the late sixties when a number of factors combined to remind women in labor unions that they were underrepresented among the decision makers in their own unions. Hundreds of cases were brought under Title VII against labor unions, presumed to be their representatives, by women workers during the late sixties and early seventies.

Federally Employed Women (FEW) was formed in 1968 to represent women employees in the federal government to "end discrimination in employment based on sex under the existing merit system." By 1973 it had 13 chapters and 2,500 members. In 1972 a United Union Women's Caucus was formed in Chicago by some 30 groups of women within trade unions. The movement to build strength for women in trade unions was at a beginning stage in the early seventies. An organization, called the National Committee on Household Employment, was formed to improve conditions for domestic workers and established in Washington, D.C. in 1970.

4. A phenomenon surprising to many observers was the development of feminism in church groups of women, which had previously confined their activities to volunteer social service efforts. The National Councils of Jewish and Catholic Women had taken stands on the Equal Pay Act decades before, but the American Jewish Congress, the American Jewish Committee and the Anti-Defamation League, and many Protestant denominations and Catholic auxiliary units began to be interested in the subject of women's rights, not only on behalf of women in their memberships, but because of widespread belief that discrimination against women generally had been bad for American society. "Women's rights divisions" developed in several auxiliary religious groups in the late sixties and early seventies. Mobilization of the millions of women represented in these groups could be a significant development in the constituency promoting women's rights lobbies in Washington and in congressional districts.

5. Minority women's organizations should also be recognized. Black women formed organizations parallel with the predominantly white professional and business groups which developed after World War I. The National Council of Negro Women, headed by Dorothy Height, was founded in 1935, and by 1970 claimed a total membership of over 4 million. It concerns itself with the "economic, social, educational, and cultural welfare of Negro women." There is also a National Association of Negro Business and Professional Women's Clubs, with 145 clubs and 15,000 members. During the late sixties, more political interest and militant spirit developed among minority women, with resulting new organizations. Some of these included the Third World Women's Alliance, which began as a Caucus of the Student Nonviolent Coordinating Committee's Black Women's Liberation Committee. It is a self-styled socialist organization favoring women's liberation, but identifying more strongly with the black movement. An umbrella group calling itself the National Black Women's Political Leadership

Caucus reported chapters in more than thirty states and held a national convention of politically inclined black women's groups in June 1973.

6. There were also public interest groups, nonpartisan, independent of religious or occupational categorization, with large memberships of women, and either a long-term or recent interest in equal opportunity for women. These included the League of Women Voters of the United States, with leagues in every state and a total membership of about 150,000. League members vote on the pursuit of issues, and do so only if there is a consensus among membership at the respective levels. They do not support either male or female candidates for public office, but have recently turned their attention to some equal rights issues. The General Federation of Women's Clubs, established in 1890, has 15,000 clubs in the United States with a total of 800,000 members, and has promoted national action in several issue areas, including equality for women. The National Consumers League, formed in 1899, and led for many years by men and women with a compassionate interest in improving working conditions for low-income workers is now primarily concerned with consumer issues. It has a membership of about 1,200 and has on its agenda some women's rights issues, such as the extension of the minimum wage to domestics. Common Cause, the organization begun by John Gardner in the late sixties, has also taken on women's rights issues, particularly ratification of the ERA.

Goals of Women's Organizations

In a survey[2] of a representative sampling of the various categories of organizations described above (about 75 groups), with about a 60 percent response, an effort was made to characterize the extent and nature of the membership and interests of the major national groups concerning themselves with women's rights issues. All but three of 45 respondents had taken strong stands (i.e., they listed them as "of major concern"), on one or more sex discrimination issues. The issues varied with the goals of the groups, i.e., equal pay and opportunity for the occupational categories represented, were naturally of major concern to the groups representing them, but more than two-thirds listed pay and opportunity equality for all women as a major concern. Somewhat less interest was shown in supporting and lobbying for specific legislation, with only about 40 percent thus engaged. These and other responses offer interesting hypotheses for further testing. The following general areas are suggested for further exploration:

1. Despite tax exempt status there are many options available for groups anxious to influence both administration and congressional policies. If 80 percent of all women's organizations in the categories listed above believe a particular issue is of major concern, why have only 40 percent taken specific policy stands on congressional bills or administration action relative to the issue? And why is the number who have elected

to educate members in such policies, and encouraged their interest in them, even smaller? A suggested hypothesis might be that there is, because of the brief history of national policy on the status of women in equal pay, job opportunity and other areas, a lag in awareness of effective strategy on the part of recently formed groups. (All of the "older"—pre-1960—organizations queried educated their members in the conduct of public policy with only two exceptions.)

2. Because most organizations did not disclose their budgets, or the percentage allocated to attempts to influence national policy, it has been extremely difficult to gauge the amount of financial resources presently at the disposal of the women's rights movement for use at the national level. Total membership of groups which consider equal pay, opportunity, vocational and higher educational opportunity, and federally supported child care to be of major, or some, concern can be counted in the tens of millions. The varying degrees of their participation in national policy needs to be explored in greater depth. The leading political activist groups are the only groups which regard all of the major sex discrimination issues as their major concern, and which support and lobby for congressional and administration action, and allocate a major share (very small) of their budgets for this activity. The potential for stimulation of additional lobbying activity among other types of groups is great, and could be ascertained with more intensive surveying techniques.

3. Certain types of women's organizations were not surveyed, including auxiliaries of predominantly male groups such as veterans organizations, women's ethnic groups, and international organizations with headquarters in the United States. Attitudes on issues of female auxiliaries in the major political parties was not explored, nor were those of mixed or predominantly male groups in public interest or other categories concerned with discrimination issues. Unquestionably the attitudes of these groups should be ascertained, if the potential of the women's movement is to be estimated accurately.

With the above limitations and needs in mind, the following limited conclusions have been drawn from the survey, as well as other data,[3] on the present state of resources of the women's movement:

1. The most active women, whether they participate as members of groups like NOW, the NWPC, or WEAL, or other kinds of organizations, attempting to influence positively the course of national policy on the status of women, are white, hold college degrees, and, if employed, hold professional or managerial positions. Supporting an estimate that they constitute more than 80 percent of active feminists are the frank admissions of their leaders, a profile of delegates to the 1973 NWPC caucus, and the results of the author's survey which disclosed that a majority of groups with equal rights a primary concern are devoted to the promotion of the careers of professional or executive

women. Public interest and religious groups also tend to have ranks filled with middle- and upper-class women with leisure time for voluntarism. Groups representing women in occupations other than professional or managerial and minority women are the smallest, both in number and in size (15 percent in the survey).

2. Existing groups appear only to be on the threshold of exerting their influence in an organized, consistent fashion, with about 40 percent pursuing all the techniques customarily employed by interest groups vis-à-vis national policy goals. Development and use of these techniques are severely hampered by a lack of funds, with only long-established organizations representing predominantly female professional occupations devoting more than a few thousands of dollars a year to educating their members on policy matters or supporting congressional, administration or judicial action.

3. Present efforts to educate women about national policy issues through detailed, frequent presentations reach no more than 50,000 women a month. Many organizations attempt to inform their members intensively on issues of specific interest to them at critical times in the formation of national policy, and, more generally and less frequently on other sex discrimination issues. With detailed information on lobbying tactics relatively scarce, the failure of organizations to attempt to affect national policy is easily explained. Allocation of more resources for "spreading the word" about congressional and administration decisions by national organizations which list sex discrimination issue areas as "major concerns" would seem to be an important consideration.

4. Approximately 80 percent of the respondent organizations presently engaged in taking policy stands on sex discrimination had either been organized or taken positions recently (from 1970 on). This fact alone may explain the lack of lobbying or related activities, since new organizations must spend a certain amount of time and resources building memberships, perfecting organizational structures, and the like before they can tackle the Hill or agency policy makers.

5. Potential participation in efforts to affect national policy is substantial. Actual participation has increased in the last two years as national activist and other organizations report increasing memberships and steadily increasing public interest. (On an average day in the New York NOW office, for example, the telephone rings every 30 seconds, with 90 percent of the calls concerning sex discrimination by local women who are not NOW members.)[4] If there is a "communication" gap there is also a "participation" gap between the upper-income, college-educated professional, managerial career women and working class women in service, blue- and white-collar occupations. The former constitute a small fraction of the working female population and a very large percentage of the activist feminist movement. The latter, particularly if one adds working class wives, makes up far more than a majority of the women in the country and a tiny fraction of the movement's membership.

Elitism in the Women's Movement

Some reasons for the present "elitist" state of the women's movement are obvious. Practical experience in organizing has been possible for "overqualified" housewives, with or without college degrees, and a desire for part-time outside-the-home-activity, who do not need to supplement the family income. Women with professional careers may not always have had the time to participate as activists in groups, but they have been able to support them financially. Women graduate students with time and energy, if little money, have been the force behind many caucuses in professional societies. Women returning to the work force after long absences for child-rearing have found themselves in low-paying jobs even if they have advanced degrees. Those remaining unemployed, in part-time work or otherwise, with free time, have also supplied cadres for the feminist movement. On the other hand the vast majority of women, whether single and working, married and working, or married and staying at home, have lacked time, and sometimes the skill, and, almost always, the money for participation in any kind of activist groups. Cultural habits, until recently, prompted many housewives to participate in neighborhood religious organizations or in auxiliary units of various kinds, which had no interest in feminism. Women trade union members have rarely become leaders or even actively participated in their unions, and have not organized women's caucuses within unions until very recently.

Lobbying by professional women's groups had a substantial impact on the 92nd Congress. Previous legislative decisions, such as the Equal Pay Act, Title VII of the Civil Rights Act, and executive action to implement the federal contract compliance program, had emerged as tools that helped middle- and upper-income working women, rather than the majority of working women their supporters intended to aid. When pressure was brought on the 91st and 92nd Congresses to extend the benefits of this legislation to more working women, the move was frustrated by the combined opposition of the president and a conservative coalition of Southern Democrats and loyal Republicans. Women already advantaged by educational and occupational status, on the other hand, were helped by the passage of legislation which extended coverage of the Equal Pay Act, Title IX of the Education Amendments of 1972, and the addition of tax deductions for child care. They were provided with additional means for fighting sex discrimination in professional and other occupations by strengthening the Equal Employment Opportunity Commission. Even though that agency had power to help blue- and white-collar women, it helped only occasionally, for reasons which have been described above.

The Need for More Participants

Professional women, aware of gains achieved in the 92nd Congress, were far from satisfied with the progress they had made, and were certainly not convinced that the movement led by the so-called "advantaged" woman had succeeded in bringing about a fundamental change in national policy on the status of women. There were the statistics, most recently emphasized by the Council of Economic Advisers Report to the President,[5] which showed that by any measurable standards, the status of women had not substantially improved. There were other indications that even educated, professional women had not experienced an improvement in their status. Ninety-eight percent of policy positions in the government, in the major political parties, and in private industries were still held by males.[6] Appointments of women to high level positions in the federal government had actually decreased during the first four Nixon years. The golden opportunity for appointment of more women during early 1973, when there were numerous vacancies, slipped by with only a handful of policy appointments. Very little was done to strengthen national programs concerned with sex discrimination.

Altruism aside, professional career women, present and potential, had an urgent need to widen the participation of all women—blue-collars, minorities, white-collars, working-class housewives—in the effort to end sex discrimination. Lobbying for issues on pay and job opportunity had to be organized among women at every income level if the national decision makers were to be persuaded that improvement in the status of women was a top item on the national agenda.

The movement for wider political participation by women took shape slowly during the early seventies. Evidence was visible in blue-collar communities, among minority women, and among white-collar working women who had been the last, it seemed, to become aware of economic discrimination. Airlines stewardesses rebelled against practices which degraded them as individuals and failed to provide them with economic security. Older women organized in the Gray Panthers, as groups of the elderly began to call themselves, formed to protest inadequate pensions and unfair social security regulations. Housewives questioned the lack of part-time employment opportunities. It was too soon to say that blue-collar, lower paid white-collar, or minority women, had become identified with leading activist organizations anywhere in the country in equal proportion to their number in the population. But evidence mounted that more such women were willing to participate, and would be increasingly more receptive to the support of lobbying movements by participating themselves, or through the power of the voting booth.

The Harris Poll

A poll taken in 1972 revealed a remarkable change in viewpoint among American women:

A swing in attitude—and a dramatic one—is taking place among women in America today. When asked in 1971 whether they favor or oppose most of the efforts to strengthen and change women's status in society today, women were almost equally divided (42 to 40 percent opposed). Only a year later, American women are voicing their *approval* of such efforts by a substantial 48 to 36 percent.[7]

The increase in the number of those favoring feminism was greatest among the 18-to-29-year-olds, and among college graduates. But those in the 30-to-39 bracket favored feminist efforts at a higher rate than before (44 to 40 percent opposed in 1971 while 49 to 36 percent favored in 1972). In the 40-to-49-year-old sector 43 to 39 percent opposed in 1971, while feminist goals were favored in 1972 by 42 to 41 percent. And even the 50s and older polled approved efforts in 1972 by 41 to 40 percent while in 1971 they had opposed such efforts by 45 to 35 percent. Women with eighth-grade educations supported feminist goals by a margin of 42 to 34 percent after opposing by a small margin in 1971; high-school graduates favored 43 to 40 percent after opposing by a large margin in 1971.

Answers to more specific questions about activist efforts to improve the status of women also emphasized the fact that women had reached new levels of consciousness about discrimination, and were ready to speak out about it. But, the survey concluded,

... the women's movement as a whole has yet to find the activist techniques to rally the majority of women, who presently look with disfavor on picketing and protest demonstrations.[8]

The poll found women increasingly eager to play more active roles politically and in the economy. First of all,

The thrust of opinion is clearly toward greater participation of women in politics. Once again, most enthusiastic is the pro-change coalition of the young, the single, the black, the poor as well as the affluent, and the well-educated.[9]

The direction that an activist movement would have to take to develop a larger constituency was evident: "As voters, women trail far behind men among Blacks, among the less well educated, and in the South and in rural areas." The coalition of those most enthusiastic for change is "most eager for increased participation in politics and for changes in the social and political structure of the country." The Harris poll comment was that "candidates who share their 'prochange' views have at their disposal untapped resources of ready and willing campaign workers. Women take the staunch position that they can be just as effective as men in politics—and, often, more so." There has been no evidence of a transference of feelings about discrimination to attitudes about other national policies or policy makers. Polling along these lines has been scanty, however. Harris found that more women were Democrats and favored a Democratic candidate for president than did men. In the course of voting in November, 1972, it appears, however, that more women voted for President Nixon than did men. More detailed polling is needed to determine the nature and degree of such transference.[10]

The January 1973 issue of *Redbook* magazine reported the results of a questionnaire on women's rights issues which they had inserted in a previous issue. More than 120,000 readers had replied, providing plentiful, if restricted sampling, of opinion from women who described themselves as political moderates, with religious affiliations and conventional attitudes in other respects. Ninety percent believed that there was discrimination against women in pay and job opportunity. Only 7 percent believed in revolutionary change to achieve equality, while one-third believed it could be achieved by working in groups. One-half confessed that the feminist movement had changed their thinking and made them more aware of discrimination. Two of every three women supported the women's liberation movement, with this proportion increasing to eight of every ten among younger women.

A Working-Class Women Study

With leading public opinion research companies just beginning to deal with basic attitudes toward discrimination in the late sixties, a comprehensive study of attitudes of ethnic working-class women undertaken by the American Jewish Committee's National Project on Ethnic America is of special interest. The report, written by Nancy Seifer, focusses on working-class women who live in northeastern and midwestern cities, often in white neighborhoods, and surrounding blue-collar suburbs. These women are part of a group of over 80 million Americans whose combined family income is between $5,000 and $11,000 a year. According to the Women's Bureau, it should be noted, of a total of 31,681,000 women in the labor force in March 1971, over 13 million were either single, married with the husband absent, widowed, or divorced, and therefore responsible for their own livelihood. Among the remaining 18½ million whose husbands were present in the household, 7½ million had husbands who earned less than $7,000 a year.[11] It is safe to assume that women who must work to support themselves, who are unemployed, underemployed, and earning less than the $7,000 a year needed for subsistence for a family of four constitute more than two-thirds of the women employed or seeking employment. It is this group which has yet to be touched to any appreciable degree by the women's movement.

Nancy Seifer points out that the late 1960s were times of change, when "working-class women were propelled into broader and more complex roles, which generated new conflicts and tensions." Changes in attitudes include, as an example, far wider acceptance of day-care centers than in the past. Increasing need for other forms of government aid were counseling service for family health and drug addiction problems, among others.

In cities like Chicago, Baltimore, Boston, and New York, working-class women have been at the forefront of community organizing to fight City Hall, and are winning an increasing number of major battles . . . .

They have succeeded at halting the construction of expressways, forcing utilities to decrease the level of pollutants they spew into the air, and fighting the blockbusting efforts of local realtors. Additionally, they have created food cooperatives to beat inflation, fought for greater safety in their schools and neighborhoods and pressured one city into changing its ordinances to allow for the establishment of more day-care centers.[12]

The women who join these movements are still the exception rather than the rule, but their ranks are growing. Baltimore Councilwoman Barbara Mikulski, with a substantial background as a self-described "ethnic" in urban community affairs, has also contributed leadership to the women's movement. Dorothy Haener, Mildred Jeffrey and Olga Madar of the UAW, have attempted to widen participation in the movement by demonstrating the benefits blue-collar women can derive from it.

It was found that working women with ethnic backgrounds believed some aspects of the women's movement to be offensive, but this did not mean that they were unaffected by the women's movement, that they did not become more independent in the context of their own lives, or that they did not support some of the programatic goals of the movement which were relevant to their own lives.[13]

Working-class women, the author points out, need help: in finding jobs and training for jobs that are accessible to them; to seek job protection through greater participation in unions (20 percent of union members are women, while only 4.7 percent are union leaders); to obtain some kind of security for the future if they stay home and maintain the household. There is increasing awareness of such problems as well as interest in solving them—for example, among caucuses within labor unions. A researcher exploring attitudes in Chicago's Southwest Side reported that:

There was virtual unanimity that wives should have as much say as husbands in making important household decisions, that women should receive the same pay as men for the same work, that a woman who does not marry can be a normal and adequate woman, and that women are as capable as men of being good leaders in science, education and politics.[14]

A few changes developed in attitudes of the offspring of the working-class, compared with those of the professional. A recent study of more than 2,500 high school girls in Texas showed that only 25 percent with blue-collar backgrounds expected to find the jobs they desired most, but they did express a greater interest in careers than similar samplings showed in previous years.

In 1970, 60 percent of the children of families with incomes between $5,000 and $10,000 were not in college. Even those in the community colleges expressed little interest in professional careers, setting their sights low for occupational goals. However, when it comes to plans young blue-collar women have for future families, there is beginning to be a difference:

The vast majority of working-class women (as well as the majority of all American women), choose marriage and a family as the highest priorities in their lives. However, while it has long been desirable and possible for many middle-class women . . . to have careers in addition to being wives and mothers, this type of life-style is just beginning to emerge as desirable among working-class girls . . . . The fact that increasing numbers of working-class girls are now seeking a higher education is radical in itself. It has also enabled them to visualize the possibility of fulfilling themselves in more than one role.[15]

In another study of freshman college students of working-class background, only 26 percent saw themselves as "housewives with one or more children," and 48 percent planned to have careers as well as to be married and have children.

Blue-Collar Cases

Further substantiating the change in attitudes on the part of lower- and middle-income working women has been the large number of sex discrimination cases brought by them under Title VII of the Civil Rights Act of 1964 and, to a somewhat lesser degree, under the federal contract compliance program. More than 20,000 sex discrimination complaints which have not been resolved by unions or companies, have been brought before the Equal Employment Opportunity Commission. Many of these still are not settled, and are awaiting litigation. Several, however, have been settled and have had substantial impact on general employment practices. The recognition by women that they had been discriminated against in employment, that there were tools offered by the federal government (as well as by state agencies) to correct such discrimination, and that they could make use of them, despite the costs and risks involved, was perhaps of far greater significance than demonstrations, consciousness-raising, and other manifestations of the feminist movement in the sixties and seventies.

Many leaders of the women's movement had been aware of the absence of blue-collar, clerical workers and of minority women in their organizations. The director of the NOW Manhattan chapter reported: "We can only take on projects that will be self-sustaining. Right now (March 1973), we are involved in a move to help secretaries and airlines stewardesses fight discrimination. But this is because a strong movement has begun among both groups. We can help them, but they have to provide the resources—both money and people—to keep it going." Working women throughout the country were actively fighting discrimination *as individuals* in the late sixties and early seventies, working their way into occupations that provided higher incomes and advancement to supervisory positions never before held by women.

In California, in 1966, Leah Rosenfeld,[16] who had been an employee with the Southern Pacific Company since 1944, bid on a job as agent-telegrapher at a railroad station in Thermal, California. She was the most senior and most qualified person bidding but one attribute—her sex—was enough to deny her the job. The company cited as justification for its action, California state law which regulated wages, hours, and working conditions for women. The job called for working more than 10 hours a day or 80 hours a week during harvest time, climbing over and around boxcars to adjust vents, collapsing railway car bunkers, and closing and sealing their doors. Applicants also had to be able to lift objects weighing over 35 pounds. Leah Rosenfeld did not object to these stipulations. The case was first decided in her favor by a district court, which ruled that refusal by the company to promote her was an unlawful employment practice within the meaning of Title VII, and that the California state law limiting the rights of women to hold such jobs was unconstitutional. The decision was upheld by the 9th Circuit Court of Appeals (San Francisco) on July 1, 1971. Individual compensation to her was probably small, since the company had abolished the job and there was a lapse of five years from the time she filed a complaint with the EEOC until the final decision by the court.

Other significant cases were won by a woman named Lorena Weeks who protested weight-lifting qualifications which kept her and all other women from advancement within the Southern Bell Telephone and Telegraph Company in Georgia;[17] by Thelma Bowe who defied the Colgate Palmolive Company's rule *and* that of the International Chemical Workers Union which prevented her from advancing in seniority because of weight-lifting and other restrictions upon women employees;[18] by Claudius Cheatwood against the South Central Bell Telephone Company because officials refused to promote her to a job as commercial representative.[19] The defendant's arguments in the latter case were typical of many used against women who wanted to advance from routine blue-collar jobs to those that were more demanding but paid more. Higher paying jobs would prevent women from qualifying, in the Company's view, because of requirements that rural canvassing for new clients might involve tire blow-outs, and attempting to collect overdue bills and emptying telephone coinboxes in bars might mean harrassment of women representatives. The company also worried about weight-lifting and produced a gynecologist to evaluate the effect of such activity on the female torso. The gynecologist concluded that from 25 to 50 percent of the female population could lift weights required by the job without damage.

Women asserted rights to a number of jobs through complaints with the EEOC, and through individual efforts. They applied, for example, for coal-mining jobs in Virginia paying $45 a day (contrasted with factory work done exclusively by women at piece rates that paid $14 a day). Such efforts proceded as legislation in 1972 paved the way for settlement of discrimination issues on a grand scale which promised to invalidate discriminatory practices at a faster pace than before. In January of 1973, the American Telephone and Telegraph Company[20] agreed to give $15 million in back pay and $23 million a year in raises to women and minority males who had experienced discrimination in job assignments, pay, and promotions. The case was marked by cooperation among government agencies, required by the new legislation. It has been pointed out that the federal contract compliance executive order can not be enforced except by a threat to withhold government contracts. In the case of A.T. & T., the government obviously cannot withhold a contract and go to another company for the same services. The case was settled on the basis of the Equal Pay Act and Title VII, while the company also agreed to abide by OFCC guidelines—fulfilling goals and timetables to end sex and minority discrimination, among other procedures. It was characterized by militancy and persistence on the part of the women involved in it. Women leaders of the Communications Workers of America who had participated in the settlement, were ready to work hard to see that enough women applied for craft jobs for which goals and timetables had been set. Verifying the trend toward greater activism[21] by blue-collar women, the EEOC reported in March 1973, that overall sex discrimination charges were increasing sharply. It estimated that they accounted for as much as 40 percent of its current case load.

Most leaders of activist feminist organizations agreed on the need to increase participation and identification with their movement among the 33 million working women and millions more housewives who, according to the Harris Poll and the Seifer Study, were more receptive to feminism than in the past, but who still neither identified with nor participated in it. There was evidence of their increased interest in the goals of feminism. Minority women were taking part in NWPC activities in urban areas as well as in its national meetings. NOW encouraged its members to initiate employment discrimination cases, and was closely involved in the A. T. & T. Co. settlement. It also has had numerous workshops devoted to economic issues at national meetings, and regularly included blue-collar discrimination in its planning and activities. WEAL has participated in the settlement of issues which affect women across the board, from employment discrimination to inability to get credit or adequate pensions. Feminists with a knowledge of history can remember times in the past when upper-class female militancy appeared to be about to be married to lower- and middle-class needs. In 1923, the divorce was sudden and almost violent when the militant suffragists under Alice Paul marched off proclaiming their unswerving and exclusive devotion to the Equal Rights Amendment, while Mary Anderson and the Women's Bureau-oriented welfare feminists stayed with protective labor legislation. Times were different in the early seventies. Cultural bias, at least among women, appeared to be yielding to the undeniable job needs of more and more single women and wives in families deprived by mounting inflation. Women were asserting themselves more, but there was evidence that they were not achieving much economically, and that the first signs that they might substantially increase their economic status were being met with stout resistance from the male-dominated establishment—all the way from the hiring halls of unions to the classrooms of universities.

The real question for the leadership of the women's movement to answer was how to capture the support of the woman who knew she was oppressed economically, so that the giant steps still to be taken toward full achievement of equality might be made by all women in time for the status monitoring which the census would provide at the end of the seventies. One major first step would be the identification of national policy agenda items that would bring full economic equality to all women, and both inform and motivate them toward greater political action.

5 An Agenda for the Seventies

By the end of the watershed 92nd Congress, the goal of complete legal and economic equality for women appeared closer for some women than others. The "advantaged" woman, the professional or executive, the educated woman or the woman able to pursue higher education, received special aid through congressional action. The disadvantaged, the working woman still not covered by minimum wage or equal pay regulations, unable to afford adequate day care for her children, elderly women trying to subsist on inadequate pensions, the sick deprived of medical care—of these, hardly any had been aided by congressional action and they were helped very little by the federal programs in progress.

Unfinished business for women included not only ratification of the Equal Rights Amendment, guaranteeing the elimination of all discriminatory laws and practices, but also action on the federal level to extend minimum wage coverage, to provide adequate child care on income-based cost to all working women, and to ensure pensions for both men and women which would adequately provide for their retirement period. Action on health care needs of women also received support—including birth control services, maternity and child care, and adequate job protection during childbearing and child rearing. "Disadvantaged women" also included individuals with incomes below the poverty level, who needed financial support and/or employment opportunities, combined with child care facilities in order to be self-supporting. Many women were paying increasing attention to the lack of opportunity for credit because of current practices and some laws which denied women everything from home-mortgage loans to check-cashing privileges in the supermarket.

Awareness of the need for stressing these specific goals was apparent as women's groups met in the early seventies. Women leaders in the National Organization for Women, Women's Equity Action League, National Federation of Business and Professional Women's Clubs, the National Women's Political Caucus, and dozens of other national groups, representing the interests of women in a variety of roles, agreed on the need for equality before the law, and for equal economic opportunity for women through federal programs that prohibited sex discrimination in pay, job, and educational opportunities. As they became more specific about their goals during national meetings in the winter of 1972-73, their increasing awareness of neglected disadvantaged women was apparent. NOW's national meeting in Washington in February 1973, for example, included several workshops aimed at blue-collar women. One was devoted exclusively to a discussion of the agreement reached with government agencies on discrimination against women and blacks by the American Telephone and Telegraph Co. There

81

was little question, however, that the so-called advantaged woman, however much she may have gained on paper from the 92nd Congress, had not been served well by the administration of programs on the books when Nixon took office.

This chapter will review a "consensus" agenda for women's rights groups as they attempted to influence the development of optimal national policy on the status of women through the administration and the Congress. In not every single instance would all feminists or related groups concur; some, obviously, assign higher priorities to certain issues than others.

Goals for Administrative Action

The White House

President Nixon acknowledged the existence of the women's movement in two ways, as his second term in office began. He appointed Anne Armstrong, formerly the top woman in the Republican National Committee, to be counselor on domestic affairs; her duties were to include overall guidance of administration action in the area of equal rights for women. There was no immediate delineation of her role; it was not clear whether her job would be similar to that outlined for a special assistant on women's rights and responsibilities in the 1970 Task Force report. In a second move, the president announced in January, 1973, the appointment of thirteen women and three men to an Advisory Committee on the Economic Role of Women.[2] The panel was to serve under the direction of Herbert Stein, chairman of the Council of Economic Advisers, to "insure that progress and change in this important area of human rights will be constructive." The yearly Economic Report of the President included a chapter on the economic role of women, marking the first time that the subject had been discussed in the report. Several women members of the committee found a draft of the report to be "unrealistic," because it implied that most women worked for reasons other than economic need. "It was written," Dr. Bernice Sandler, Director of the Project on the Status and Education of Women of the Association of American Colleges, declared, "about working women solely in terms of problems they create, rather than their contribution to the economy."[3]

The chapter on women was rewritten in time for the publication and transmission of the report to the Congress, as it convened. Citing the Employment Act of 1946, which had established the CEA, the report defined its goal of "maximum production" as meaning "that people should be able to work in the employments in which they will be most productive," and added that the goals applied "equally to men and women." It then explored the role of the committee relative to discrimination in the work force. No mention was made of specific implementation of the Nixon Task Force recommendations. The committee was to "meet periodically with the Chairman of the Council of Economic Advisers, providing a forum for the interchange of information, ideas, and points of view." As its name suggests, it has no decision-making powers; it lends advice to an advisory committee. The report states that "Because the function of the Council of Economic Advisers is to advise the President on a wide variety of economic issues, its association with the committee will ensure that the interests of women will be represented in economic policy decisions." No steps have yet been taken by this committee that will have the impact the Nixon Task Force suggested would be needed to advance national policy on the status of women.[4]

The chapter in the Economic Report of the President presents a number of statistics on the economic status of women. They are taken from the 1970 census and uniformly show that economic discrimination against women persists, despite the federal programs and other tools which have been developed to try to overcome it. There is a tendency to restate arguments which representatives of women's groups believe to have been settled already. For example, the report points out that only 6.4 percent of working women with children under six used group care centers, according to a 1965 survey.

Some have attributed the low use of day care to a failure of the market to provide a service that would be utilized if financing were available. Others have interpreted it as an indication that the true demand for institutional care is low. Whether institutional day care provides the best use of dollars spent on child care has yet to be established.[5]

The legislative history of the Child Development Bill in the 92nd Congress is filled with endorsements of properly staffed day-care centers from more than 20 national organizations, including the AFL-CIO, the U.S. Catholic Conference, the National Council of Churches, the National League of Cities, and the U.S. Mayors' Conference. Several studies, including one by the National Council of Jewish Women, "Window on Day Care,"[6] had affirmed the kind of inadequate care provided in unlicensed facilities for children of low-income families.

The following suggestions for White House policy are items on the agendas of almost all of the women's rights organizations. They are brought together here, as a consensus of action items; many organizations assign priority to some recommendations and not to others—and there are a few on which all the organizations with equality for women as one of their goals might not agree.

Decision-makers in the White House, whether designated as domestic policy counselors or as a "super-cabinet", should be clearly assigned duties that relate to policy on the status of women. Such assignment of duties should be the occasion for a statement by the president regarding his administration's commitment to legal and economic equality for women.

The various units of the Executive Office of the President should be assigned functions related to the execution of the president's commitment. The Office of Management and Budget should be adequately staffed, and its examiners briefed on the various programs designed to provide equal opportunity for women. Machinery for this exists, but needs to be implemented.

The Interdepartmental Committee on the Status of Women, which did not meet during the first Nixon administration, and which was designed to review and to evaluate the progress of federal departments and agencies in advancing the status of women on a continuous basis, should meet at least twice a year and make its reports and recommendations known to the public.

The major departments and agencies which have most to do with the status of women—Labor, HEW, EEOC, Justice, the Civil Service Commission, as well as all other agencies and departments—should be staffed by policy officials who openly and firmly are committed to equal opportunity for all.

Full use should be made of the EEOC Coordinating Council, which consists of the Secretary of Labor, the Chairman of the EEOC, the Attorney General, the Chairmen of the Civil Service Commission, and the Commission on Civil Rights, and which has responsibility for developing and implementing agreements, policies, and practices regarding the enforcement of equal employment opportunity legislation, orders, and policies. On or before July of each year the Council should send to the president and to the Congress a report, together with recommendations for legislative and adminis-trative changes.

The Civil Rights Commission has an implicit coordinating and explicit corrective role vis-à-vis administration policies. Its intentions to fulfill its recently enlarged mandate with regard to sex discrimination should be made clear. Its reviews of policies should include all of the programs listed below, and should be in-depth appraisals of their successes and failures. The commission should also explore na-tional goals for women, and revise them in accordance with their responsibilities.

The Treasury Department, which supervises administration of the 1972 Revenue Sharing Act, should review guidelines regarding sex discrimination as they apply to the expenditures of revenue-sharing funds by state and local governments, and strengthen them so that national policy of equality for women is not dissipated at the local level.

White House recruiting for policy positions should include consideration of women for every policy position; appointment of women should advance well beyond its present 1 percent level.

All government statistics recording information about people should be divided into male and female categories and, under each sex, by the accepted minority subhead-ings.

Talent banks maintained by a number of organizations should be consulted by the government for policy and middle-grade positions for appointments of qualified women.

Federal Employment

Significant changes were made in the equal employment opportunity pro-grams in the federal government by the EEO Act of 1972. The act not only gave statutory authority to the program, which had been based on an executive order, but also provided court remedies for aggrieved employees dissatisfied with the decisions made by their agencies or the Civil Service Commission on their complaints. Agency heads are also required to submit an annual EEO plan to the Civil Service Commission for approval. Such plans must include provision for the establishment of training and education programs, and a description of the qualifications of the principal officials responsible for carrying out the EEO program. Agencies have been instructed by CSC regulations to develop specific "action items", using goals and timetables and avoiding generalities.

On the basis of suggestions in the report, and critical information provided by FEW, the Nader report, and other studies, the following are considered to be significant items for the women's lobby agenda in the 1970s.

The Federal Women's Program should be adequately staffed, and the seriousness of its mission emphasized, along with those of the coordinators in each department and agency. Accountability methods should be strengthened and clarified.

The commission has delayed release of statistics on the numbers of employees, divided by sex, at each grade level, despite the fact that such figures are kept on computer tape within each agency and department. Such statistics should be released to the public promptly each year, one or two months after the cutoff date of October 31.

Action plans for each agency and department should be published, as should the annual evaluation of it made by the Civil Service Commission.

Since the 1972 Equal Employment Opportunities Act provides for consultation with "interested individuals, groups, and organizations" and the "soliciting of recommendations from them," this official channel should be used by all groups monitoring the progress of the EEO program. Specific suggestions should be prepared and referred to the CSC.

Reductions in force should be monitored for their possible and actual effect on federal women employees. Attention should be drawn to those which deal unfairly with women.

Affirmative action plans should include detailed instructions on employee utilization. These plans should be monitored from this and other points of view, such as the level of resources committed to the program, career counseling available, and manager training provided.

Department of Labor

The department has three major women's programs under its guidance. During the reorganization period of the second Nixon administration, it was unclear for a period of months who would be appointed to the policy positions below the level of secretary. In view of the presidential decision to keep a tight control over policy appointments, there was a hiatus in decision making at the top department level during the first months of 1973, when no policy appointments for the Employment Standards Administration were made. The effect of this on policy as it related to equality for women was certainly not positive. It appeared that the three women's programs would remain under the guidance of the Employment Standards Administration (barring a possible decision by Anne Armstrong to suggest different White House policy along these lines). Presidential or congressional action to change the situation appeared remote.

The Women's Bureau

The Women's Bureau budget has remained static in dollar terms for a number of decades. At a time when there are an increasing number of women in the work force with no other government agency able to answer questions on a variety of subjects that are of particular concern to them, the resources of the bureau should be increased to match demand for its service function.

Services should include sponsorship of conferences or workshops on a number of subjects, including pay and working conditions of household workers, unemployment of women (particularly younger women), discrimination by labor unions, the dignity of certain occupations (including service employees), applications for newly opened craft jobs and apprenticeships, and expertise in the use of other federal programs that relate to women.

To back up such services, the bureau should engage in research on various problems to be faced in the seventies by working women, including equal pay and opportunities, vocational and professional training, child-care facilities sponsored by private industry and subsidized by the federal government.

Office of Federal Contract Compliance

The long delay in the issuance of guidelines on sex discrimination by the OFCC, its hesitant and somewhat inconsistent use of sanctions, its obscure position at less than bureau level in the Labor Department hierarchy, all have been the subject of criticism by the Civil Rights Commission and groups concerned with the rights of minorities and women.

The Civil Rights Commission should do an in-depth study of the OFCC from the standpoint of its effectiveness in administering sex discrimination guidelines, the appropriateness of its recent reorganization, and its budgetary needs as it affects all phases of the program, including its supervision of all the contract agencies.

Over 250,000 companies hold government contracts and therefore must not discriminate against women in any of their employment practices. Women's organizations should encourage reports from their field organizations on the effectiveness of contract compliance in companies in their areas. Affirmative action plans are supposed to be available to employees or to the public, and to be given publicity in the community generally.

The success of OFCC action within companies may be judged by (a) whether minorities and women are being underutilized in desirable job classifications to which they have previously been denied admission; (b) the kind of corrective action available to employees; (c) goals and timetables the plant has established for craft and managerial positions; (d) how well policy has been publicized in the plant and throughout the community; (e) whether its effectiveness is being measured within the plant by officials in charge; (f) whether organizations of women locally or within union and/ or plant are giving support to the plan; (g) what is being done to eliminate explicit and implicit discriminatory practices.

Equal Pay Act

Procedures for recovering back pay and gaining appropriate increases, when discrimination has been found under the Equal Pay Act, have generally been prompt and effective. The act was extended to professional, executive, and administrative personnel in 1972 under the Education Amendments. Women's groups promoting equal economic opportunity will be monitoring the program's continuing effectiveness, which was generally regarded as acceptable during the Johnson and first Nixon administrations.

Administration staff should be increased to meet additional cases expected because of the added coverage of the Act.

Field units of national organizations should be aware of proper procedures for filing complaints, and should publicize these where investigations have revealed discrimination.

HEW Office for Civil Rights

Groups of professional women and students on campuses throughout the United States, stimulated by the leadership of the Women's Equity Action League, have taken the initiative in encouraging the monitoring and enforcement of contract compliance regulations by colleges and universities. The Office for Civil Rights at HEW has been slow to enforce contract compliance before action was taken by women's groups, despite the fact that the EO prohibiting discrimination by those holding contracts with the federal government had been in effect since 1968. Individual employees of institutions of higher learning are now covered by the Equal Pay Act, as well as by the Equal Employment Opportunity Commission. Legislation in 1972, extending prohibitions against sex discrimination, increased OCR prerogatives substantially.

New guidelines, awaited since passage of the Education Amendments in July 1972, should be examined upon their publication and their effectiveness monitored in practice.

There should be an immediate review by the Secretary of HEW, of backlogged campus contract compliance complaints, with prompt notice given of intention to reduce the backlog, as well as to hold precontract reviews, whenever appropriate.

Campus women's groups should be contacted prior to complaint reviews, and their testimony taken into consideration prior to such reviews.

All campus units should check on the availability of affirmative action plans on their campuses. Problems should be reviewed by national organizations, and progress toward solutions periodically noted.

The consequences of affirmative action planned, and taken, should be regularly monitored by campus feminist groups.

Equal Employment Opportunity Commission

As previously noted, the EEOC received considerable increase in authority and coverage by 1972 legislation. Such increases should be noted and publicized by various action groups. They include extension of coverage to (a) state and local government employees; (b) employers and labor organizations with 15 or more employees or members; (c) educational institution employees.

Complaint procedures have changed and EEOC can now bring court action against a company when conciliation fails. Action against state and local agencies can be brought by the attorney general.

Guidelines on revised coverage and procedures should be obtained from EEOC regional offices and reviewed;

Backlogs presently overwhelm the proper functioning of EEOC in every region, and are expected to become even more serious under EEOC's mandated expansion. Management must be improved, and budget increased to reduce the backlog;

Women's groups cannot expect employers or labor unions to take initiative in enforcing the act within their companies or organizations. It is important to uncover grounds for justified complaints, and to assist individual women in the filing of them, monitoring the results for the benefit of the individual, and other women, who might be affected by them;

EEOC has investigatory, research, and service functions in addition to its enforcement authority. Use of these functions as they apply to sex discrimination should be reviewed, needs surveyed, and requests made for individual projects by EEOC.

Other agencies that should be monitored include:

1. The Defense Department, because of discriminatory practices involving women in the services, and because it dispenses so many government contracts;
2. The Treasury Department, for its role in operating revenue-sharing, which will affect a vast number of functions at the local level;

3. The Commerce Department, because of its Office of Minority Business Enterprise, should be pressured to give aid to women seeking to establish businesses, including financial assistance for pilot or demonstration projects, providing information, etc.;
4. The U.S. Postal Service, because it has the largest number of employees and the fewest number of women in supervisory positions, despite the fact that one-third of the nation's postmasters are women.

The Congress

Congress, which has the power, on one hand, to help provide legal equality for women, and, on the other, to end economic discrimination against them, faced major decisions on women's rights issues at the beginning of the seventies. Having passed the Equal Rights Amendment by wide margins, both Houses would be required, upon its ratification, to pass legislation which would bring all federal statutes in line with its provisions. On the economic side, Congress would be asked to monitor programs already established, to see that they had sufficient funds to handle demand for their output, and to pass legislation in a number of areas—some involving newly developed issue areas, and others that had been on committee calendars for years.

The more specific and, at the same time, more numerous powers granted to the Congress by the Constitution, combined with the very great increase in the number and complexity of issues facing it, have made lobbying within that body in recent years a complex and all-consuming task. Greater demand for action on an issue generally brings a mixed blessing—a proliferation in the number of groups and individuals ready to go into action on the Hill. At the beginning of the 93rd Congress, women's rights issues were in competition with many of more immediate and dramatic impact. In January 1973, the avowed intention of the president to use his prerogatives to curb spending and end domestic programs, dominated the Congress despite the confirmed resistance of a majority (but not, apparently, a sure two-thirds) of the members of the legislative branch. The president was willing to fund at least some of the programs dealing with discrimination against women—in particular, the studies that were to be undertaken by the Civil Rights Commission. All of these programs, expenditures for which would probably total less than $70 million annually, were a very small slice of the federal pie. Women's rights groups, concerned with particular programs designed to enforce national policy about equality for women, also gave priority to legislative decisions on health, welfare, and child care. Although many would not acknowledge its direct relevance to equality, which was presumed to be part of national policy regardless of the economic state of the nation, the specter of reduced federal expenditures and a resulting loss in employment opportunities, haunted their efforts as the 93rd Congress began.

In addition to opportunities for influencing national policy through substantive legislation, women's rights groups had to check Presidential appointees to see how committed the new occupants of sensitive positions in HEW and the Department of Labor, and the contract compliance agencies would be. They would also be concerned about the number of appointments that would go to women. There was no evidence of an increase in high-level appointments of women as replacements in subcabinet level positions were made in the spring of 1973.

Congressional Investigations

The investigatory powers of Congress, which had yet to be related to sex discrimination, could be used in connection with a resolution introduced by Congresswoman Martha Griffiths (D., Mich.) in the 93rd Congress, to "ascertain and identify those areas in which difference in treatment or application, on the basis of sex, exist in connection with the administration and operation of those provisions of law under the respective jurisdictions (of all of the standing committees of the House of Representatives)." House Resolution 108, introduced early in January 1973, and referred to the Committee on Rules, provided that each standing committee submit to the House during the current session of the Congress a preliminary report of its studies, together with appropriate recommendations, and then submit to the House, not later than October 1, 1974, a final report with recommendations. It authorized hearings by the committees and did not apply to the Committees on Appropriations, House Administration, Internal Security, Rules or Standards of Official Conduct.

There were other suggestions for use of the congressional investigatory and oversight function:

If statistics continued to show marked disparity in pay and opportunity for women, hearings should be held by appropriate committees in either House on the general topic of unemployment of women in areas or occupations where opportunity is particularly rare, or where opportunities for employment potential have been denied.

Oversight hearings are in order for two or, perhaps, three programs: EEOC because of its great backlog of cases, OFCC because of the delays in promulgating and implementing guidelines, and HEW's Office for Civil Rights because of its long failure to conduct contract compliance reviews on college campuses efficiently and promptly.

Major items on an agenda for investigatory hearings, preparing for legislation, include (a) Income tax payments, as they affect women; (b) Credit availability of all kinds—consumer, home, and business—related to women; (c) Aid to Families with Dependent Children payments, and other social security benefits related to the health and well-being of female recipients.

Major Substantive Items

Minimum Wage

Most of the major women's groups considered renewed efforts to pass a minimum wage bill a priority item as they developed strategy for the 93rd

Congress. Offers to organized labor to work together were accompanied by requests that officials of the AFL-CIO, and certain affiliates, cease their opposition to the ratification of the Equal Rights Amendment in those states which still had not ratified by the beginning of the legislative sessions of 1973. Other than that, the women's groups had to demonstrate a certain amount of native strength for a grass-roots lobbying effort throughout the country, congressional district by congressional district, which would be sufficient to overcome the resistance of Congress to the minimum wage bill favored by both women's groups and organized labor, as well as a number of other organizations, including civil rights groups. There was room for bargaining on certain items, but women's groups indicated their intention of holding fast to the extension of the minimum wage for domestics while labor would not be budged from its opposition to the reduction of the minimum wage for those under the age of 21.

Previous grass-roots campaigns offered help to women's groups as they explored specific ways to achieve their priority congressional items. A legislative fight for the amendment of the Federal Labor Standards Act, one that took place in 1955, offered some interesting parallels. A succinct, yet detailed, description of labor's successful grass-roots effort by Gus Tyler suggests possibilities for mobilizing today's activist women. Labor leaders that year made major strategy decisions which not only succeeded in increasing the minimum wage (from 75 cents to $1 an hour, with no extension in coverage), but acquainted many local leaders and members of unions with lobbying techniques which were to become useful in later years. Tyler points out,

... the Joint (Minimum Wage) Committee was finally persuaded to use the broadside, rather than the pinpoint, attack by two other considerations: (1) the trade-union structure is such that it is, in a national campaign, much more difficult to try to influence individual Congressmen than to express a nationwide opinion of all of Congress; (2) in preparation for future elections, it was considered advisable to involve as many union members as possible in order to convert the minimum-wage effort into one great class in civics.[7]

Labor needed, in 1973, an infusion of new activists. Women's groups needed, not only expansion of their constituency among the women to be aided by the minimum wage bill (as well as the other priority legislative matters outlined above), but improvement of their lobbying techniques. In particular, the women's lobby needed to be flexible enough to produce an ad hoc organization planned to follow congressional-district lines. In this way grass-roots demand for legislation could be stimulated and individual congressmen acquainted with the developing groundswell for minimum wage, child care, and other matters of immediate and urgent need for women.

Such a move, identifying women's issues with the needs of whole communities, would provide strength to the feminist movement, which it appeared to lack, and which was particularly noticeable during the fight for ratification of the ERA. The movement, thus, had everything to gain from mobilization for passage of FLSA amendments during the 1973-74 Congress.

Women's groups were instrumental in the passage of the Minimum Wage bill by Congress in 1973 with extension of its provisions to household workers. Provisions of the bill which then went to the President were similar to the 1971 Senate version (page above).

Child Care

Support for child-care legislation comes from a number of different groups: social service organizations, many of them religious in orientation, organized labor, educators, welfare recipients, minorities, and feminists. The president's veto of comprehensive child-care legislation in 1971 had been followed by Congressional efforts to pass a bill that might meet with White House approval, but had not mustered sufficient strength for passage. The Congress, however, extended Office of Economic Opportunity programs toward the close of the 92nd Congress, and increased the financing of the Headstart program.[8] Legislation provided that participation without charge was to be limited to families with incomes below $4,320 a year. The Secretary of HEW was to make provision for the establishment of fees for families with higher incomes. At the same time, child care was provided through the social services authorized in the Social Security Act (H.R. 1—an amended version of the president's welfare proposals). Appropriations for child care were expected to total about $1,350,000,000 in fiscal year 1973 and $1,097,-000,000 in fiscal year 1974.

The groups which had supported the vetoed Child Development Act were not satisfied with the OEO child-care provisions for a number of reasons. Most of the provisions for a broad range of educational, nutritional, and health services for children in need of preschool care had been removed and no replacements made for standards, or for extending care on a pro-rata basis for higher income levels for all working parents. The results of congressional action which limited (because of the presidential veto) child-care funding to OEO, through Headstart and to the Social Services Provisions of the Social Security Act, were a source of increasing concern. On the one hand, the president was dismantling OEO, and, on the other, HEW Secretary Caspar Weinberger was issuing regulations for the use of Social Security funds (approximately $700,000,000 or more than half the total money assigned to child-care facilities), incorporating many of the features of H.R. 1, which were considered to be highly undesirable.

Protest over the regulations dominated the child-care scene in early 1973. Senator Walter Mondale (D., Minn.), sponsor of the vetoed Child Development bill, found five major faults with the regulations:

1. The regulations sought to repeal provisions for the use of privately contributed funds to make up the required local- or state-match of funds;
2. The regulations repealed the use of contributions for the state- and local-match of such items as donated space, equipment or services. This alone would end many day-care programs;

3. Services for former welfare recipients were limited to 3 months, and barred aid to potential welfare recipients with incomes of more than 1 and 1/3 times the welfare income level.

... under this new definition, former welfare recipients appear to be denied eligibility for day care just after that day care has permitted them to find employment and leave the welfare rolls. Unable to afford adequate care for their children, they are likely to be forced back on welfare. This is precisely the kind of mixed-up incentive system which traps people in poverty; [9]

4. The proposals remained "silent on the critical question of standards for federally assisted day care." As Judith Asmuss, of the Washington Research Project Action Council in Washington, said; "The argument in the last Congress concerned ways in which to improve standards for child care. The administration through its regulations suggests that now the argument must deal with whether to have any standards at all." [10]
5. Since the regulations required quarterly—and in some instances, more frequent—reports on each person receiving aid, they threatened to "drown the social services program in red tape."

As the new session of the Congress began, proponents of child care, Senators Mondale and Javits, and Congressman Ogden Reid introduced measures which would nullify the regulations. The Senate bill was supported by 40 other senators and the House bill by 76 congressmen. Individual congressmen, from a number of different areas, reported very heavy mail from constituents protesting the cutbacks which resulted from the new regulations, which in many areas had the effect of reducing social services, including child care, more than fifty percent. The administration itself, apparently, counted on a substantial cutback since it had asked for only $1.9 billion for all of the social services, while Congress had authorized $2.5 billion. The assumption was that regulations would lessen the need for the larger sum.

Social Services Cutbacks

The social services cutback affected, in addition to funding for child care, aid to the elderly, mental retardation, juvenile delinquency, and other services. Opposition to it came from social welfare leaders, the Council of State Governments, organized labor, and a number of other groups, including feminist organizations. Their program called for speedy amendment of the regulations so that funds for child care would be freed on the same basis as they were before, or on a basis more acceptable to those who supported the child-development bill of the previous session of Congress. Specific goals which they approved, and which were part of the legislation that died in the Senate late in 1972, include:

1. Authorization of almost $3 billion over a three-year period for child-development programs for children from low-income families. This

would have included $1.2 billion for fiscal year 1974 and $1.6 billion for fiscal 1975;

2. A local governmental unit or combination of units of general local government (of at least 25,000 population), an Indian tribal organization or a public or private non-profit agency could be designated a sponsor of child-development and family-service programs to apply for a grant from HEW. Each sponsor was to establish and maintain a child and family service council, half of its membership to be drawn from parents with children participating in the programs;

3. Families of four or more with an annual income of $4,320, or less, to receive free services—with a sliding-fee scale for parents with higher incomes, based on ability to pay;

4. Funds were reserved for programs for the children of migrant agricultural workers, children on federal and state Indian reservations, and handicapped children;

5. The Secretary of HEW was to promulgate a set of program standards to apply all child-development programs;

6. The authorization of funds for Headstart was repealed, effective July 1, 1975. The Office of Child Development in HEW was to be the principal administrative agency for the programs.

Pensions

The 92nd Congress attempted to deal with unsatisfactory aspects of private pension plans. The Welfare and Pension Plan Act of 1958 had required that administrators of plans report annually on the operation of funds. It did not provide for such protection to pensioners as "vesting"—permanent assignment to employees of accumulated pension benefits after a certain period of time, should they leave the company or for "portability"—taking accumulated pension funds from one job to another. The Senate Labor and Public Welfare Committee reported an administration bill in September 1971 designed to correct certain abuses which was then referred to the Finance Committee, at the request of its chairman, Russell B. Long (D., La.).

Hearings conducted by the Senate Subcommittee on Labor of the Committee on Labor and Public Welfare in 1971 and 1972 highlighted some of the abuses prevalent under present private pension plans.[11] In 1972, hearings were conducted in several states to emphasize the experiences of individual workers who had worked decades for private companies only to find themselves without a pension when plants closed or moved, or if they were forced out before the time required to earn the pension had passed. Women over 65 are among the least protected and the poorest citizens—earning a median income of $1,397 per year. The issue was particularly significant to women for many reasons: they are even more concerned about "vesting" than men, since they are apt to move in and out of the labor force for extended periods of time because of childbearing and child rearing. "Portability" applies to them for the same reason—since their return to the work force means a return to the same company only occasionally. They are predominantly employed in jobs which presently do not provide pensions; and they tend to outlive men, and, thus, are dependent on pensions for a longer period of time. Women who do not work, but have maintained households, should be protected as well as those who have worked, in the view of the legislation's supporters.

The Senate Labor Committee bill (reintroduced in the 93rd Congress) contained the following major provisions:

1. Employees in private companies which employed more than 25 persons were to be vested with 30 percent of their accumulated pension benefits after eight years of service, with an additional 10 percent to be vested each succeeding year, so that a worker would be entitled to his or her full pension after 15 years' service;
2. Employers were required to fund all normal service costs of the pension plan annually, and to set aside, within 40 years of the act, sufficient assets to pay the claims of all vested workers;
3. A federal pension plan termination insurance program would be established and employers required to insure all unfunded vested liabilities;
4. Guidelines were to be set for the voluntary establishment of a central clearinghouse through which employees of participating companies could transfer vested pension benefit credits from one employer to another;
5. Stricter regulations were to be established for the selection and conduct of pension plan administrators and more detailed disclosure of the funds' operation;
6. An Office of Pension and Welfare Plan Administration within the Labor Department was to be set up to supervise private plans and enforce regulations established by the act.

An administration plan, proposed in a message to Congress by President Nixon on 1971 and 1973 would have provided minimum federal standards for the vesting of pension plan benefits as a condition for tax-exempt status for such plans; raised the limit on tax-deductible contributions to pension plans made by the self-employed for themselves and their employees, to 15 percent of the first $50,000 of earned income, for a maximum deduction of $7,500 (an increase from the present limit of 10 percent of earned income or $2,500), and would have permitted another advantage to the self-employed by providing a tax deferral for personal funds set aside for retirement to a limit of 20 percent of earned income or $2,500. AFL-CIO's spokesman, Andrew J. Biemiller, called the administration's proposal "a new tax loophole for the wealthy under the guise of pension reform." The "rule of 50," the administration's vesting formula would have guaranteed an employee whose age and years of service with a company totaled 50, with 50 percent of pension plan benefits. Every qualified worker would have been guaranteed an additional 10 percent each succeeding year; after five years he would have been entitled to his full pension. Biemiller charged that the annual cost "required to fund a pension benefit to a person at or near age 50 is very high," and many employees would be unwilling to underwrite this cost.

A variety of opinions was expressed during hearings held by the Senate Labor and Public Welfare's Subcommittee on Labor in 1971. The National Council of Senior Citizens supported the committee bill as coming closest to the recommendations made by the 1971 White House Conference on Aging. Other representatives of retired men and women backed the legislation. For the most part private industry supported the Nixon version of the legislation, although the Finance Committee, insisting upon acquiring jurisdiction of the bill, stripped it of almost all of its important provisions. The vesting right was removed, employers did not have to set aside enough funds to pay pensions, the insurance plan, which would have guaranteed pensions in the event of cancellation or firm bankruptcy, was dropped and voluntary portability was also cancelled. The administration, with strong allies in the Finance Committee (chaired by Russell Long) preferred both a weaker bill and one that would be in the hands of the Finance rather than Labor Committee.

Credit

Just as it was responsible for pressure for equal economic opportunity for women, the increasing presence of women in the work force had much to do with growing demands for equality in granting credit.[12] A wide variety of practices discriminated against women; their correction was on the collective agenda of women's groups:

1. The wages of young married women were either not taken into account when a married couple was considered for a mortgage, or else were counted on a pro-rata basis as one-fourth or one-half of the total. Women were asked to put in writing the kind of contraceptives they used as a means of guaranteeing that they would not have children. In some instances, men were asked to present written proof that they had had vasectomies:
2. Women, who had worked and paid bills from their own earnings, had credit cards taken away without explanation when they divorced, or when they married;
3. Married, self-supporting women were unable to obtain credit if their husbands were poor credit risks even though they were separated;
4. Women who wanted loans to start businesses were told they would have to have their husband's written approval, and that he would be responsible in case of default.

These, and hundreds of other instances of separate standards for men and women, though the women in question had worked for long periods of time and had not defaulted on loans or could be called poor credit risks, came to light under the investigations of hundreds of local women's groups during the early seventies. The Center for Women Policy Studies in Washington received a grant from the Ford Foundation for a comprehensive study of the problem of the relative lack of credit privileges for women. As the center pointed out, in a preliminary report, it was "an issue that concerns every woman and cuts across all economic, social, and racial lines."

While there were few states and no national laws that discriminated against women (by insisting that credit institutions provide different requirements for loans for women than they do for men), and grass-roots efforts to reverse centuries-old practices seemed to be achieving some results, there was, nevertheless, widespread pressure on Congress to pass laws prohibiting discriminatory practices in the granting of credit.

Legislation in response to this need was introduced by Congresswoman Bella Abzug (D., N.Y.), in the form of three bills at the beginning of the 93rd Congress (Referred to the Banking and Currency Committee). They would prohibit discrimination on account of sex or marital status in any federally-related mortgage transactions; they included reporting requirements for such transactions.

They amend the Truth in Lending Act to prohibit discrimination by creditors against individuals on the basis of sex or marital status, with respect to the extension of credit. A similar measure was introduced in the Senate by Harrison Williams to prohibit discrimination by any federally insured bank, savings and loan association or credit union against an individual on the basis of sex or marital status in credit transactions and other activities.

The Equal Consumer Credit Act, introduced by Representative Margaret Heckler (R., Mass.), would make it a crime for creditors to discriminate on the basis of sex or marital status in issuing charge accounts or credit cards.

Health Insurance

Major efforts to pass comprehensive health insurance, the Kennedy-Griffiths bill, and an administration proposal, failed in the 1971-72 Congress. Women who do not work, and who are not covered by their husband's policies, must depend, like all the unemployed and self-employed, upon purchasing individual policies. Such policies are more expensive than those supplied by most firms, and by the government, in terms of their cost and the benefits they provide. Both the Kennedy and administration bills sought to correct inadequacies in health care: the former through a national-health-insurance system which would be administered by the federal government and financed by payroll taxes as well as by general federal revenues, and the latter by private insurance for employees and by using federal-family-health insurance for low-income families.

While most women's groups favored improved health care, they had not lobbied intensively for it in the 92nd Congress. It appeared on the agendas of more groups in 1973, particularly on NOW's, which pointed out that most present health insurance did not cover adequately costs frequently borne by women for contraception, maternity care, and abortion. Women's groups were also concerned about provision for maternity care and the fact that childbearing should be included as a health disability in employer plans. Plans were under way to put pressure on the 93rd Congress for such measures, as women's groups were once more allied with organized labor in its support for the Kennedy-Griffiths bill.

Other legislative items supported by major women's groups included a bill that would provide benefits for both men and women who have remained at home to maintain a household; reduce from 20 to 5 the number of years that a divorced woman must have been married to allow her to collect benefits from her former husband's earnings; compute social security earnings by combining husband and wife's benefits; provide that remarriage does not terminate benefits nor reduce their amount. Further amendments to the Social Security Act appeared to have an uncertain chance in the 93rd Congress because of the length of time spent on major revisions in the previous session of the legislature. Amendments to the Internal Revenue Code were introduced which would provide full benefits of income splitting enjoyed by married individuals to all unmarried individuals, and to remove rate inequities for married persons, when both are employed.

Also, a bill that would encompass both legal and economic discrimination, first introduced in the 92nd Congress as an omnibus bill, which would put into law most of the provisions of the Nixon Task Force's provisions on Women's Rights and Responsibilities. The bill, in the 93rd Congress, included the prohibition of sex discrimination in public accomodation, public education, federally-assisted programs, and housing. A bill introduced by Congresswoman Abzug would amend the Civil Rights Act titles where applicable. Since some liberal Congressmen did not want to run the risk of providing an opportunity for a borderline conservative coalition to overturn the Civil Rights laws, features of the legislation were also introduced independently of them.

The Family Planning Services and Population Research Act (PL 91-572) expired on June 30, 1972. Its extension was to be considered in the 93rd Congress by the Public Health Subcommittee of the House Interstate and Foreign Commerce Committee, and the Senate Labor and Public Welfare Committee's Human Resources Subcommittee. It was expected that bills to provide family-planning services to low-income women, and to increase contraceptive research would also be considered. The president has proposed that these measures be included in a revenue-sharing measure. Research has been urged by many women's groups in the improvement of contraceptive techniques. Several sponsor the creation of an Institute for Population Sciences to conduct such a program.

The Married Women Federal Employees Act was introduced by Representative Griffiths and referred to the Education and Labor Committee of the House. It would provide equality of treatment with respect to married women federal employees in connection with compensation for work injuries and other purposes. She has also introduced a bill that has been referred to the Foreign Affairs Committee, which would provide equality of treatment for married women employees under the Foreign Service Act of 1946.

The Ms. bill, introduced by Congresswoman Abzug, would prohibit any instrumentality of the U.S. from using as a prefix to the name of any person any title indicating marital status.

With priorities set and ready for lobbying for minimum wage, child care, credit, and a series of other bills, major women's rights groups prepared strategy and looked for increased resources in order to gain more from the 93rd and 94th Congresses than they had from the 92nd. They planned to prod the administration on the one hand about major bottlenecks concerning the enforcement of legislation, and, on the other, to seek allies in an effort to bring economic equality to women—and, inevitably, to become involved in greater protection for all the economically disadvantaged.

6 Strategy and Tactics for the Seventies

The information presented in the previous chapters can be used to guide feminist lobbyists toward a reasonably swift and certain achievement of optimal national policy on the status of women. Armed with a full knowledge of federal programs, their failures and their possibilities, and an itemized national agenda for future administrative and legislative action, the strategist who keeps abreast of domestic policy making on the federal level should be able to develop accurate guidelines for the achievement of immediate and long-range goals. Activists for equal rights have not yet developed an overall strategical or tactical plan for this purpose. This chapter will attempt to bridge the final gap between commitment to economic and legal equality for women and its achievement.

Successful strategy for feminists would appear to depend on following a series of steps familiar to the movers of national policy in any issue area:

1. Coordinated strategic and tactical planning by the major groups which have as their priority the elimination of sex discrimination;
2. Maximization of the resources of the feminist movement in terms of participants and voter support, funds for activities such as research, lobbying, campaigning within interest groups and political parties, and the development of data helpful to the course of national policy in the administration, the Congress, and the courts;
3. Concentration on goals with the greatest possibility of achievement and the support of the largest number of women, and which will be advantageous to the whole movement;
4. An aggressive search for alliances among other interest groups which will maximize opportunities to influence decision makers in the Congress and the administration;
5. Identification of all possible access points in order to facilitate continuous two-way communication with agency staffs and congressional committee personnel, with the goal of expressing need for federal programs and pressuring for their optimal output;
6. Utilization of access points to power through participation in political-party and interest-group leadership positions.

Coordinated Planning

The need for coordinating efforts to influence national political decisions on the status of women has been apparent since the movement began to develop strength in the late sixties and early seventies. Many attempts have been made to satisfy the need. Open discussion sessions have been held, such as those conducted by ERA Ratification Council while state legislatures consider approval of the Amendment. Other ad hoc groups have formed to pool lobbying efforts. Representatives of some thirty-five to forty women's organizations, with headquarters in the Washington area, have had the opportunity of meeting from time to time to get to know each other and to *discuss* cooperation, but so far they have not practiced it on a regular basis.

In times of crisis, i.e., sudden requests for a testimony at a hearing, for votes in Congressional committees or on the floor, distress signals have produced cooperation but, again, this is not synonomous with continuous, coordinated action.

Some organizations, noting the lack of continuous activity on the part of ad hoc groups, have cried out for the ball and run with it. Lobbying is, however, a team sport and must be played that way to win.

It is suggested that all organizations with a primary goal of influencing national policy on the status of women form an ad hoc, unstructured council, whose members will represent and relate to a number of similar groups for purposes of collective, optimal strategic planning. They should meet frequently, as needed, and make specific plans for action.

Unanimity in all respects is not to be expected. Maximization of resources is to be earnestly sought, however, or the whole feminist movement is apt to suffer bruising, if not annihilating, setbacks. Egos of individuals and of groups will have to be sacrificed for the common good, the true hallmark of mature and responsible political action.

What does the unstructured council do?

It reaches (hopefully) binding (but not irrevocable) decisions for major organizations on all of the matters outlined below, offering opportunity for flexibility (emergency tactics) as well as optimal strategic planning. It should operate on a basis of mutual loyalty which avoids mutual criticism or self-aggrandizement for the sake of unilateral advancement. It should correct mistakes quickly and expect efficient performances from its participants.

Maximizing Resources

Support for mutually agreed upon goals must be obtained from a maximum number of women voters and participants.

All leaders of women's groups must be continually aware of the potential value of support from large numbers of women with a variety of life-styles, incomes, and education, who have common interests in ending discriminatory practices and laws. The Harris poll said it—a majority of women approve feminist goals but are repelled by certain feminist tactics.

Emphasis on "image" in a campaign to gain political power is all-important, as the pollsters have shown. All of the other attributes of successful campaigning (research, newsletters, well-timed political action) may not be able to counter an image that goes contrary to the concepts with which the majority of women identify.

The media has tended not to take the feminist movement or its goals seriously. A responsible press has emerged in the last few years, however, with conscientious reporters like Eileen Shanahan of the *New York Times,* Isabelle Shelton of the *Washington Star-News,* Marlene Cimons of the *Los Angeles Times,* among others, dealing with national women's rights issues as they would with any other major policy area. At the NWPC Houston meeting in February 1973, some women worried that the long wrangling over structure might result in a bad press, the kind of "put-down" that many reporters had practiced in the past. Observers were ready to believe that the women's rights issue had come of age when a male wire-service reporter commented: "There's nothing that unusual about this kind of meeting. I've seen plenty of men get into worse messes than this." Most reporters at the Houston meeting did treat the Caucus convention objectively.

An image that will draw maximum support depends partly on issues chosen for action. Everything else being equal, maximum support depends on selecting the issues with the maximum appeal. (see Chapter 5).

Secondly, image depends on a sound, well-researched approach; mature and serious presentation of issues on a continuous basis surpasses the flash-in-the-pan demonstration, whose intentions in any case may be distorted in the local press.

Thirdly, many women's rights leaders, the products of universities and colleges, with professional backgrounds and an identification with liberal causes, have to learn to identify more with working women and housewives who do not share their backgrounds. Blue-collar women who have begun to participate in the movement are a small minority, and their interest may easily be snuffed out by the attitudes of those who have been in the vanguard of the movement. Acceptance of identification with all other women may be hard for the woman who has struggled against heavy odds to achieve professional status. The extent to which the woman leader will be able to identify with less advantaged women very likely, in the long run, will determine her successful leadership.

Funds as a Resource

It is difficult to estimate the amount of money that has gone into recent efforts to change national policy concerning the status of women. All participants and observers would have to agree that, in comparison with other similar domestic issue areas and, indeed, with the amount that was invested in the fight for woman's suffrage during a similar time span, the sum has been very small—probably no more than a few hundred thousand dollars.

Many professional staffs have served on a volunteer or pin-money basis, a practice which is not only degrading but self-defeating. Since the object of the movement has been to open up jobs for skilled women, successes in the movement have tended to deprive it of professional help.

A cultural habit of "thinking small" has afflicted many women. They collect "small" and they give "small." Unquestionably, this attitude is rooted in sensibly founded feelings of financial insecurity, but if feminist goals are to be achieved at a faster pace than they have been to date it is an attitude that must change. Individual women with incomes in the middle or upper brackets will have to get into the habit of contributing to causes they believe in and that will, in turn, profit them. This is a habit shared by most male members of professional and business groups. Organizations should consider hiring professional fund-raisers or permitting fund-raisers to keep a percentage of contributions as salary. Timidity in setting or striving for fund goals can only hold back achievement.

Research Data

An enormous amount of data has been collected about and in the name of the feminist movement. Bibliographers find it difficult to keep up with scholarly efforts to assess attitudes, evaluate textbook references to women, describe the history of feminism, the pay differential between men and women, opportunities for women in management and so on. There is, however, a yawning gap between present scholarship and the need for material that will advance feminist attempts to influence national policy on the status of women.

Social science research tends to concentrate its efforts on itself—i.e., women professionals in various disciplines have turned the spotlight on the subversion of their own goals or used the techniques they have studied on the status of women in other professions to reflect on the low status of women everywhere—*in the professional world.*

While scholarly efforts should have support, it is important to note that they have failed thus far to deal in depth with the attitudes of working women and housewives toward discrimination. They have also failed to provide a means of acquainting these women with facts about equal rights. Thus, there exists a two-fold task for women's rights leaders: to direct research efforts toward these as yet unstudied areas, and to see that the information is put to use in the movement.

Selection of Goals With Maximum Appeal

Some widely acceptable goals for women have been suggested in previous chapters. They include equal pay (extension of minimum wage to all workers), equal employment opportunity (hiring, promotions, benefits), federally supported comprehensive child-care facilities, and greater old age and health protection for women. A majority of women have important stakes in each of these issue areas.

Achievement of these goals hinges on decisions made by the administration, the Congress, and, in some instances, the courts. In given regional areas, at particular periods of time, there will be greater utility in stressing some issues rather than others. Women's groups should be able to relate to all of them, however, and appeals for membership should not only include descriptions of discriminatory practices but the ways in which the persistent activity of women can alleviate the situation.

There are issues which should be emphasized at the discretion of the group and its leaders. This does not mean "self-censorship"; goals that members wish to adopt because they have deep feelings about their justice should not be denied. These include issues that are controversial for many women, such as abortion reform, or that may seem trivial to some, such as the use of Ms. as a form of address. Compromise is an acceptable device for achieving goals that would not be gained any other way. It need not mean a sacrifice of principles.

Alliances With Other Interest Groups

There are present and potential allies for women's rights groups among organizations pursuing similar or related goals. These include organized labor, civil rights groups, certain public interest and welfare-oriented groups such as those concerning themselves with aging or disadvantaged people. Alliances with many other groups are always possible, either on an ad hoc basis for a particular issue, or as part of a long-range cooperative effort.

The word "alliance" implies a sharing of mutual tolerance among groups, as well as a respect for goals and attitudes that may involve differences which the participants do not find to be intolerable. Each group that is male-dominated may reflect attitudes toward the feminist movement which will stand in the way of full cooperation. Two things will correct this situation: sensitivity on the part of women leaders to such feelings and the reasons for them, and a demonstration of solidarity and effectiveness on the part of women's groups which will make them worthwhile, and indispensable, allies.

Minorities

In the sixties, the fight to end discrimination in employment, education, and public accomodations was all about minorities and hardly about women at all. Women—minority women and white women—are sometimes a threat to males among minority groups who have gained from the civil rights movement of the sixties. One fear, that minority males are being asked to share a slender piece of establishment pie that has been set aside for them with women, and mostly white women at that, could be replaced with the conviction that the pie can be made big enough for all individuals to share— whether it represents education to qualify for jobs, jobs themselves, or other criteria of economic equality.

If this basic fear can be overcome and identification of purpose achieved, there are still problems of communication to solve. Establishment of mutually loyal feelings, customarily achieved in the course of a long struggle with all parties on the same side remaining faithful to the cause and therefore to each other, are prerequisite to a firm alliance. Both minorities on the one side and women's organizations on the other (with Black women sometimes standing uncomfortably in the middle), agree that there is a long way to go before it can be said that this kind of relationship has been formed between the civil rights and feminist movements.

One of the clues to the situation is the development of self-confidence on both sides. Minorities, particularly Blacks, have achieved a substantially higher percentage of participation in Congress and in state legislatures in accordance with their number in the population than have women. (Minority women are generally included in both figures and thus are counted twice. Among Black state legislators they have fought hard battles to win ten percent of the total.) There is no substitute for the strength that an increase in the number of minority men and women, and white women, in public office can bring to both groups. This means that a truly meaningful alliance on such matters as mutual support for offices, support on other issues, and so on can be of inestimable advantage to both groups.

Communication between the Black movement and the feminist movement should occur at several levels, and should be frequent, taking place at all the important phases of a lobbying effort and about all issues in which each group shares a substantial stake.

Organized Labor

The women's movement and organized labor were allied together in a lobbying effort for the strengthening of the Equal Employment Opportunity Commission, the fight for the minimum wage and child-care legislation in the 92nd Congress, and were poles apart on the ERA. While almost all of the women who lobbied for the labor-supported legislation considered the ratification of the ERA crucial, efforts to persuade the AFL-CIO leadership to abandon its opposition to ratification, which had had a powerful effect in several of the states which turned down ERA, were fruitless as state legislatures met in the winter and spring of 1973.

Two developments must take place before a more equitable alliance can be achieved. Labor, 99 percent male-dominated, has to be convinced of the efficacy of the political strength of the women's movement, and, secondly, the latter must gain strength within the local and even national leadership of the trade union movement itself.

Optimal strategy for the women's movement, therefore, should include a more equitable relationship with unions which would maximize the ability of the women's groups to supply more grass-roots support for mutual lobbying goals than it has heretofore been able to provide. It also means that bridges have to be built between feminist activist and rank-and-file women labor union members. This task should be made easier by the recent development of women's caucuses within unions, and by a more positive attitude toward equal rights with labor organizations.

Social Welfare Groups

Volunteer organizations, sometimes the "surrogates" of the disadvantaged, associated with religious groups, or descendants of the Progressive movement, and voluntarism, etc., have identified very strongly with many equal rights issues, despite the seemingly opposite approach they take from many feminist groups. (Many of the latter are, in fact, much opposed to voluntarism.) Groups like the National Councils of Jewish Women and of Catholic Women have a long history of support for equal pay for women and for federally supported child-care facilities. There is an opportunity through association on every level to provide mutual support for these and other issues.

These groups provide the clues to a broad-based feminist movement among groups yet to be mobilized. Millions of women may thus be involved in grass-roots lobbying support for all the major goals of the women's rights movement. There is evidence that many of their members have reached a better understanding of its militant phase.

Other Sources of Support

The Nixon cutbacks in social services, dismantling of the Office of Economic Opportunity, and insistence that the domestic budget be sacrificed for continued high expenditures for defense, have threatened far more groups than the present allies of the women's movement named above. The beginning of the new administration found scientists, university presidents, mayors of cities large and small, educators, community action groups, a wide range of public interest groups, all searching for ways to gain strength to maintain the programs and services they believed to be necessary for the survival of tolerable living conditions everywhere in the United States.

While the president's strategy made lobbying for specific goals for women's rights issues (and all others) a more complex task than it had been before, feminist groups were given the opportunity to supply grass-roots efforts to fight presidential cutbacks for community-oriented programs, and to develop skills and support they might have lacked otherwise. Signs pointed toward the need to begin a nationwide effort to organize on the congressional-district level in order to capitalize on the potential support of the threatened groups.

Access Points in the Administration

Staff members of federal equal opportunity agencies—EEOC, Employment Standards Administration in the Labor Department, Civil Rights Commission, and the Office for Civil Rights in HEW—and political activists in the movement are natural allies. The extent and nature of the alliance depends on a number of other factors: whether or not the administration hierarchy has given its blessings to the program, the attitude of bureaucrats and their willingness to join hands with clientele to improve program output, and the continued appraisal of their efforts by women.

Frequent and meaningful communication between activists and agency personnel is of first-rank importance. The lifeblood of the agency may well depend on the enthusiasm for the program interest groups can stir in Congress via grass-roots efforts in congressional districts. Excessive backlogs in the handling of grievances, inefficient supervision of contract compliance reviews by regional program personnel, should be the occasion for action by those who have been the victims of agency failures to carry out congressional mandates.

President Nixon provided women's rights groups with two more opportunities to promote their interests within the administration by appointing the new committee on women's equality issues to advise the Council of Economic Advisers, and by naming Anne Armstrong, former co-chairperson of the Republican National Committee to act as a White House counselor. Her duties were to include the general supervision of women's equality programs. The degree to which either appointment would provide a conduit to the makers of national policy in the executive branch was uncertain. It would no doubt be worthwhile for women's groups to explore these avenues, particularly when crucial administration decisions are in the offing.

Administration officials with the power to make life-or-death decisions about agency programs are more impressed by evidence of constituent support if it is channeled through congressmen than if it comes from individuals. And while congressmen tend to be impressed by any evidence of interest in a federal program on the part of a voter in their district, it is more important to have evidence of support for improvement in a program from a number of constituents.

Monitoring equal employment programs (see Chapter 2), serves the immediate purpose of maximizing help for women who need it and of guiding the efforts of those who want to add to agency resources to increase their output. Accumulated evidence of shortcomings, brought to the attention of administration leaders, the press, and appropriate congressmen, can help to correct deficiencies. All programs should be closely followed with this in mind.

Congress

Hill lobbyists customarily come to be on close terms with staff members of committees handling legislation of interest to them. In turn, they can be useful sources of information for committee staff members. Because of the complexity of most issues facing Congress, including those that have to do with sex discrimination, it would make sense to have some groups specialize in particular issue areas, or even subdivisions of these issue areas. All aspects of a subject should be studied: output of federal programs, progress of legislation, allied interest group activity, White House policies, etc.

Timing is an essential ingredient for successful lobbying, as important as the achievement of maximum grass-roots support. In the course of coordinating lobbying activity, women's groups must be aware of the progression of each major item on the legislative calendar, and time their preparation of testimony, grass-roots level activity and other efforts associated with it.

Every Woman a Lobbyist

The truly national character of the interest in the women's rights movement has been well established. Southern women thought to be too ladylike for activism, New England women thought to be too independent and rural, ethnic women thought to be too subject to male domination, have participated in one phase or another of the women's movement. Women in all walks of life have responded to calls to help bring more freedom in job choice, higher pay, and greater political power. These regional and local units need more leaders, more participants and more consistent direction from national leaders.

Suggestions for increasing CD organizational activity include the distribution of legislative "handbooks" listing information about congressmen and congressional procedure. Lobbying tips should be provided, such as the advantages of writing particular kinds of letters, of personal visits on the occasion of the congressmen's return to their home districts on holidays.

The handbooks should contain detailed information on developing media publicity, the names of other local groups which have taken national positions on equal rights issues, and related state and local problems, such as ERA ratification or implementation. Inserts on timely issues can be mailed periodically. Resources should be maximized in a situation like this to avoid duplication of "newsletters" by national organizations. The suggested council should take on the responsibility of coordinating this effort. Many of the current national women's organizations have operated similar kinds of activities and should be able to provide help. They should also be able to assist in the development and circulation of the handbooks which can, of course, be provided in a variety of forms, so long as they contain essential information and have as their goal the development of congressional district organizations.

Political Parties and Interest Groups

Policy makers in the political parties and in interest groups have a role to play in changing national policy on the status of women. Women should be in leadership positions in both beyond their present low participation rate.

Feminist groups should relate to the women who presently participate as rank and file activists in both political parties, no matter how insupportive of equal rights these party workers have been. Women have been among the most experienced fund raisers, the hardest working grass-roots organizers and many times the most loyal to party principles in both parties. Many of them would seek leadership positions if they had encouragement and support from women activist groups. If such an effort is identified as a party take-over, of course, resistance will be aroused.

Women need to assert leadership roles in special interest groups like labor organizations and others which have an affinity for equal rights goals. This will no doubt occur more frequently as they increase their number in unions and in professional ranks. Caucuses and even separate auxiliary women's units have very limited impact now. It will become increasingly important for women to take part in the power structure of presently male-dominated professional and public interest groups and labor unions.

Women in all modern countries have been taught to forego interest in the use of political power. Even rudimentary prerogatives, such as voting, have been denied to them. The road to decision making has been opened for women only grudgingly, after fierce struggle.

There was evidence on all sides in the United States in the late sixties and early seventies that an increasing number of women understood the nature and effect of sex bias, and that attempts to end it had involved them in the political process nationally and locally as they had never been involved before. They were learning about their government, about how to participate in democracy, meeting in small groups and large conventions to settle on a national agenda for women's rights, and to agree on the way to achieve it.

Despite gains made in the sixties and in the 1971-72 Congress, statistics continued to affirm what most working women knew already: there was a distance to go if national policy was to be effective in ending sex discrimination. Through cultural habit women tend to be plodders, used to routine tasks, not shrinking from them, especially if they see a purpose in them. Women are humble in the face of new knowledge and new tasks. Note in both political parties, for example, the prevalence of workshops when large groups of women activists convene. Note the absence when male politicians get together. Women feel compelled to learn before they believe themselves to be ready to do.

Participation in elections, and in local, state, and national lobbies formed to deal with Congressional and state legislation, and in other moves to put pressure on policy makers at the national and state level, has provided training grounds for cadre and leaders of the political side of the women's movement. How national policy is formed and what can be done to change it has been outlined on these pages. The rest of it, the forgetting of cultural lessons, the keeping up with changing laws and policies, the campaigning—whether it be for a candidate or a law—is in the hands of those who want to replace the oligarchical characteristics of a male political establishment with a democracy that recognizes and provides for the optimal contributions of all of its people.

Notes

Chapter I

1. The Declaration of Sentiments written and adopted at the meeting of feminists has been extensively reprinted. Stanton, Anthony, and Gage, pp. 70-73.

2. Ibid.

3. Executive Order 10980 Establishing the President's Commission on the Status of Women, *American Women*, 76.

4. President's Task Force on Women's Rights and Responsibilities, *A Matter of Simple Justice*, iii.

5. Caroline Bird's *Born Female* was a pioneer effort along these lines.

6. Ethel M. Smith, *Toward Equal Rights for Men and Women*, 34.

7. For a review of economic discrimination from the aspect of the role of private industry as it has affected the employment of women, see Jerolyn R. Lyle and Jane L. Ross, *Women in Industry: Employment Patterns of Women in Corporate America* (Lexington, Mass.: Lexington Books, D.C. Heath and Co., 1973).

8. Dean D. Knudsen, "The Declining Status of Women: Popular Myths and the Failure of Functionalist Thought," *Social Forces,* 48:186. Used by permission, U. of No. Car. Press.

9. Manpower Report of the President, transmitted to the Congress, March, 1972, 171-2.

10. Knudsen, op. cit., 187.

11. Juanita Kreps, *Sex in the Marketplace: American Women at Work*, 40.

12. National Education Association, Research Division, *Salaries Paid and Salary-Related Practices in Higher Education,* 1971-72, 11.

13. Civil Service Commission, *Study of Employment in the Federal Government, 1971,* computed from Table E.

14. Department of Labor, Women's Bureau, *1969 Handbook on Women Workers,* 11.

15. Department of Labor, Women's Bureau, "Why Women Work," compiled from Bureau of Labor Statistics, Employment and Earnings, January, 1972.

16. Sar Levitan, et al., *Human Resources and Labor Markets,* 409.

17. Department of Health, Education and Welfare, *Projections of Educational Statistics, 1981-2.*

18. Department of Commerce, Bureau of the Census, "School Enrollment in the United States: 1972 (Advance Data)", Current Population Reports.

19. Johnston and Knapp, "Sex Discrimination by Law: A Study in Judicial Perspective," *New York University Law Review,* 46:737.

20. Ibid., 737.

21. Brown, et al., "The Equal Rights Amendment: A Constitutional Basis for Equal Rights for Women," *Yale Law Journal,* 80:923. Reprinted by permission of The Yale Law Journal and Fred B. Rothman & Co., also pp. 964, 961, and 946.

22. For a sound legal review of the ERA, see Marguerite Rawalt, "The 'Equal Rights for Men and Women Amendment' is Needed," *Women Lawyers Journal,* 59:4.

23. Jane R. Chapman and Margaret Gates, co-directors of the Center for Women Policy Studies, Washington, D.C., will issue reports on a study of "Women and Credit," which has been financed by the Ford Foundation.

24. Kanowitz, *Women and the Law: The Unfinished Revolution,* 18.

25. Brown, et al., op. cit. 964.

26. Ibid, 965. Cf. Carolyn Engel Temin, "Discriminatory Sentencing of Women Offenders: The Argument for ERA in a Nutshell," *American Criminal Law Review:* A Symposium, 11:355ff.

27. Ibid, fn 226, 961.

28. "Note. The Victim in a Forcible Rape Case: a Feminist View," 11. *American Criminal Law Review:* 335. Reproduced by permission of the American Criminal Law Review and the American Bar Association, 1973.

29. Seneca Falls Declaration, op cit.

30. Brown, et al., op. cit., 80:946.

31. Citizens' Advisory Council on the Status of Women, *The Equal Rights Amendment and Alimony and Child Support Laws,* 6.

Chapter II

1. Commission on Civil Rights, *The Federal Civil Rights Enforcement Effort. A Report of the United States Commission on Civil Rights, 1971,* 1.

2. President's Task Force on Women's Rights and Responsibilities, *A Matter of Simple Justice,* 1970, 2.

3. Catherine East, the council's executive secretary, who combines an impressive knowledge about federal involvement in sex discrimination with a remarkable ability to write and lecture on this and other aspects of the women's movement, has made, with the help of a capable staff of one, a substantial contribution to the development of national policy on the status of women.

4. Commission on Civil Rights, *The Federal Civil Rights Enforcement Effort: One Year Later,* November, 1971, 208.

5. Task Force on Women's Rights and Responsibilities, op. cit., 22.

6. Ibid., v.

7. *United States Organizational Manual,* 1969-70, 318. During the Nixon years the functions of the Women's Bureau were steadily eroded. The 1972-73 *Manual* has a one-sentence description of the bureau's function: "The Women's Bureau is responsible for formulating standards and policies which shall promote the welfare of wage earning women, improve their working conditions, increase their efficiency, advance their opportunities for professional employment, and investigate and report on all matters pertinent to the welfare of women in industry."

8. Elizabeth Duncan Koontz, "Women at Work: The Women's Bureau Looks to the Future," *Monthly Labor Review,* June 1970, 5.

9. U.S., Congress, House, Committee on Education and Labor, *Discrimination against Women: Hearings before a special subcommittee on Education of the Committee on Education and Labor, House of Representatives, on Sec. 805 of H.R. 16098,* 91st Cong., 2d sess., 1970, 692.

10. Ibid., 450.

11. Department of Labor, *58th Annual Report* (fiscal year 1970), 17. There were other "reorganizations" involving the Women's Bureau. Cf. Employment Standards Administration Memorandum to all ESA Personnel, dated September 24, 1971 and Secretary's Order No. 4-72 dated January 27, 1972.

12. U.S., Congress, House, Committee on Education and Labor, *Equal Pay for Equal Work. Hearings before a select Committee on Labor of the Education and Labor Committee on H.R. 8898 and HR 10226,* 87th Cong., 2d sess., 1962, passim.

13. Morag MacLeod Simchak, "Equal Pay in the United States," *International Labour Review,* 103:550.

14. Department of Labor, Employment Standards Administration, *Minimum Wage and Maximum Hours Standards Under the Fair Labor Standards Act,* 1973, 7.

15. Schultz v. Wheaton Glass Co., 421 F. 2d 259 (3rd Cir. 13 Jan. 1970), *certiorari* denied, 398 U.S. 905 (1970).

16. Department of Labor, Employment Standards Administration, op. cit., 11.

17. Civil Service Commission, *Toward Equal Opportunity in Federal Government.* (Brochure, no page numbers.)

18. Helene S. Markoff, "The Federal Women's Program," *Public Administration Review,* 32:144.

19. *Federal Personnel Manual,* Chapter 713, Subchapter 2-6c.

20. Markoff, op. cit., 32:147.

21. Daisy Fields, "A Case of Non-Feasance," *The Bureaucrat,* 1:227.

22. Federally Employed Women, *FEW Conference Report,* passim.

23. *The New York Times,* September 1, 1972.

24. Federally Employed Women, op. cit., ii.

25. Ibid., 146.

26. M. Weldon Brewer, Jr., *Behind the Promises: Equal Employment Opportunity in the Federal Government,* VI-1.

27. Ibid., VI-34.

28. *Federally Employed Women,* op. cit., passim.

29. Mary Eastwood, *Fighting Job Discrimination: Three Federal Approaches,* 12.

30. Brewer, op. cit., 4.

31. Ibid., III-10.

32. Interview with Helene Markoff.

33. *The Washington Star-News,* March 8, 1973.

34. Civil Service Commission, *Study of Employment of Women in the Federal Government, 1969, 1970* and *1971.* It should be noted that the figures for 1971 exclude not only 22,500 employees in agencies with fewer than 2500 employees, but also the entire Postal Service.

35. Citizens' Advisory Council on the Status of Women, "Chronology on Inclusion of Sex in Executive Order 11246," undated memorandum prepared by Catherine East.

36. President's Task Force on Women's Rights and Responsibilities, op. cit., 19.

37. Quoted in Mary Eastwood, op. cit., 11.

38. Doris Wooten, "The Issue is Compliance," *Contact,* Fall, 1972, 13.

39. Commission on Civil Rights, *The Federal Civil Rights Enforcement Effort—a Reassessment,* January 1973.

40. Ibid., 71.

41. Ibid., 71.

42. Interview with Dr. Sandler.

43. Dr. Bernice Sandler and Sheldon Elliott Steinbach, "HEW Contract Compliance—Major Concerns of Institutions," Special Report of the American Council on Education, 2.

44. HEW, Office for Civil Rights, *Higher Education Guidelines, Executive Order 11246.*

45. Quoted in Association of American Colleges, Project on the Status and Education of Women Bulletin, November 1972.

46. J. Stanley Pottinger, "The Drive Toward Equality," *CHANGE Magazine,* October, 1972, 24.

47. Interview with Peter Holmes.

48. Leo Kanowitz, *Women and the Law,* 106.

49. Equal Employment Opportunity Commission, *Annual Report, 1972.*

50. Catherine East, "What the Government Will Require," unpublished paper, 1972, 8.

51. Ibid., 4.

52. Mary Eastwood, op. cit., 8.

53. Commission on Civil Rights, *Federal Civil Rights Enforcement Effort, 1971*, 98.

54. Commission on Civil Rights, *Federal Civil Rights Enforcement Effort, A Reassessment, 1973*, 78ff.

Chapter III

1. Major legislation and Public Law Numbers are as follows:
Equal Employment Opportunities Act—P.L. 92-261
Title IX, Education Amendments of 1972—P.L. 92-318
Comprehensive Health Manpower & Nurse Training Amendments Acts—P.L. 92-157
Civil Rights Commission—P.L. 92-496
Tax Deductions for Child Care—P.L. 92-178
Federal Employees Benefits—P.L. 92-187
Social Security Benefits—P.L. 92-603
Refer to *WEAL Washington Report*, Report Number 8, December 1, 1972, Ellen Sudow, ed.

2. See also, AFL-CIO Department of Legislation, *Labor Looks at the 92nd Congress*, 113.

3. The Ford Foundation has made a grant to the Cornell University School of Industrial and Labor Relations to find out why women have failed to assume leadership roles in trade unions, in proportion to their numbers as members.

4. *Congressional Record*, House, October 6, 1971, H 9245.

5. George P. Sape and Thomas J. Hart, "Title VII Reconsidered: The Equal Employment Opportunity Act of 1972," *George Washington Law Review*, 40:824 is an excellent review of the legislative history of the effort to add cease and desist power to EEOC's enforcement authority, and the implications of the new authority it did receive. Copyright © 1972 by the George Washington Law Review.

6. Ibid., 843.

7. Summary from Conference of Senate Committee on Labor and Public Welfare and House Committee on Education and Labor, 92nd Cong., 2d sess., *Equal Employment Opportunities Legislation* (Comm. Print 1972).

8. Sape and Hart, op. cit., 40:889.

9. A critique of the higher education legislation similar to that done by Sape and Hart for the EEOC bill is, unfortunately, lacking. See Association of American Colleges, Project on the Status and Education of Women, fact sheets and chart. Also Conference of Senate Committee on Labor and Public Welfare, and House Committee on Education and Labor, 92nd Cong., 2d sess., *Report to Accompany S 659*, (Report No. 92-798) 221-2.

10. U.S. Congress, House, Committee on Education and Labor, *Discrimination against Women*, op. cit.

11. Association of American Colleges, Project on the Status and Education of Women, fact sheet.

12. Guidelines to implement the legislation had not been promulgated by HEW in time for review for this book.

13. The extension of Fair Labor Standards equal pay to women professional, executive, and administrative employees "sneaked through" via the education act, in effect, before administration forces in Congress could muster sufficient strength to oppose it.

14. U.S. Congress, Senate, Committee on Labor and Public Welfare, Report on S. 1861 (S. Rept. 92-842). Summary from Committee Report. The Minimum wage bill reported in June, 1973, was not essentially different insofar as it affected women workers.

15. Senator Walter F. Mondale (D., Minn.), *Congressional Record,* 92nd Cong., 2d sess., Vol. 118, No. 21, Feb. 17, 1972. See also Senator Jacob K. Javits, (R., N.Y.), statements in press releases, Feb. 24 and 28, 1972.

16. Alice M. Rivlin, "A New Public Attention to Pre-School Child Development," *Washington Post,* Dec. 1, 1971.

17. President Richard M. Nixon, Economic Opportunity Amendments of 1971. Veto Message (House Document No. 92-48).

18. U.S. Congress, Senate, Committee on the Judiciary, *Civil Rights Commission,* Report on HR 1265 2 (S. Rept. 92-1006), 3.

Chapter IV

1. Data on women's organizations has been provided by the list of organizations compiled by Betty O. Dabagian, Programs and Systems Division, Office of Contract Compliance, Department of Defense (available on request); organization publications, participation by the author in regular and annual meetings, and inquiries addressed to their leaders.

2. The respondents were asked to state, first, the extent of their concern (major, some, little), and the year of their involvement in:
Equal employment opportunity for all working women;
Equal employment opportunity for a particular job or professional category;
Equal pay for all working women;
Equal pay for selected job or professional categories;
Equal educational opportunities for women;
Child care facilities for all working women supported by federal government.
Second, they were asked for their policies toward specific bills in the 92nd Congress (favored, no action, opposed):
OEO extension, including child care;
Mondale comprehensive child care bill;
Extension of Equal Pay Act (Minimum Wage);
Equal Employment Opportunity Act;

Higher Education Bill (Education Amendments of 1972).

Third, they were asked for their policies toward the Nixon administration—whether they supported or took no action on the following policies, and whether the Nixon administration had been satisfactory or not satisfactory:

More appointments of women to high and middle level positions in government;

Administration of Title VII of the Civil Rights Act;

More diligent enforcement of the Equal Pay Act, and of enforcement equal employment programs.

Fourth, they were asked to indicate to what extent their organizations had encouraged members to influence public policy by taking public positions; testified at hearings, and supported sympathetic candidates.

Fifth, they were asked if they had supported or filed suit in court discrimination cases.

Finally, they were asked to estimate the percentage of their budget used for lobbying purposes.

3. Data supporting the composition of support for activist organizations include a delegate profile collected at the NWPC Convention in Houston in 1973, and estimates by other groups of membership characteristics.

4. Interview with Jackie Starkey, office manager, New York City Chapter of NOW.

5. Council of Economic Advisers, *Economic Report of the President, 1973,* Chapter 4.

6. Cf. Committee on Post Office and Civil Service, Senate, United States Government Policy and Supporting Positions, 93rd Congress, 1st sess, passim.

7. Harris, Louis, and Associates, *The 1972 Virginia Slims American Women's Opinion Poll,* 2.

8. Ibid., 8, and Section 1, passim.

9. Ibid., 22.

10. Ibid., Section 2, passim.

11. Department of Labor, Women's Bureau, fact sheet "Why Women Work," 1972. See also William Spring, Bennett Harrison, and Thomas Vietorisz, "Crisis of the Underemployed," *The New York Times Magazine,* Nov. 5, 1972, 42.

12. Nancy Seifer, *Working-Class Women in America,* American Jewish Committee National Project on Ethnic America, 165 East 56th Street, New York, N.Y. Availability from the committee anticipated by the time of publication of this book. Page references not available.

13. Ibid.

14. Ibid. Material on the Southwest Side was taken from Kathleen McCortt, "Politics and the Working-Class Woman: The Case on Chicago's Southwest Side."

15. Seifer, op. cit.

16. Rosenfeld v. Southern Pacific Co., 293 F. Supp. 1219 (C.D. Calif., 1968).

17. Weeks v. Southern Bell Tel. and Tel. Co., 408 F. 2d 228 (5th Cir. 1969), which revised 277 F. Supp. 117 (S. D. Ga., 1967).

18. Bowe v. Colgate Palmolive Co. and International Chemical Workers Union, 416 F. 2d 711 (7th Cir. 1969).

19. Cheatwood v. South Central Bell Tel. Co., 303 F. Supp. 754 (S. D. Ala., 1969).

20. The settlement was signed by the company, the EEOC, and the Labor Department on January 18, 1973. See *The New York Times,* Jan. 19, 1973. cf Equal Employment Opportunity Commission, *Unique Competence: A Study of Equal Employment Opportunity in the Bell System,* Dec. 1, 1971.

21. Equal Employment Opportunity Commission, *Annual Report,* 1972.

Chapter V

1. A meeting of activist groups was held at the headquarters of the National Woman's Party, 144 Constitution Avenue, N.E., Washington, D.C., on January 30, 1973 to discuss the political agenda of the feminist movement. Present were representatives of WEAL, NWPC, NOW, the National Black Women's Political Leadership Caucus, the Women's Lobby, the National Woman's Party and the National Welfare Rights Organization. The agenda described in this chapter reflects their suggestions and criticisms, but is not intended to identify specific policies. The meeting was sponsored by the Federation of Organizations for Professional Women.

2. *The New York Times,* Jan. 7, 1973.

3. Ibid., Jan. 18, 1973.

4. Council of Economic Advisers, *Economic Report of the President,* 90.

5. Ibid., 111.

6. National Council of Jewish Women, *Windows on Day Care,* passim.

7. Gus Tyler, *A Legislative Campaign for a Federal Minimum Wage* (1955), 15.

8. See U.S. Congress, Senate, Committee on Labor and Public Welfare, *Comprehensive Child Development Act of 1971, Hearings,* and *Headstart and Child Development Legislation, 1972,* passim (both).

9. Statement by Senator Mondale, *Congressional Record,* Vol. 119, No. 29, Feb. 26, 1973.

10. Interview by telephone. See Washington Research Project Memorandum to Social and Rehabilitation Service, HEW, March 9, 1973, re: Comments on Proposed Social Services Regulations.

11. Several case histories are described in U.S. Congress, Senate, *Examination of Private Welfare and Pension Plans, Hearings* before the Subcommit-

tee on Labor of the Committee on Labor and Public Welfare, 92nd Cong., 2nd sess.

12. Rep. Bella S. Abzug (D., N.Y.), "Sex Discrimination in Bank Loans and Consumer Credit Transactions," *Congressional Record,* Vol. 118, No. 83, May 23, 1972.

Bibliography

Bibliographical Material

Hughes, Marija Matich. *The Sexual Barrier: Legal and Economic Aspects of Employment, 1970.* (With 1971 and 1972 Supplements). Available at Box 702, 2116 F Street N.W., Washington, D.C. 20037.

Rosenberg, Marie Barovic and Len Vincent Bergstrom, *Women and Society: A Critical Review of the Literature with a Selective Annotated Bibliography.* Beverly Hills, Ca.: Sage Publications, 1973.

Women Studies Abstracts (quarterly). Available at P.O. Box 1, Rush, N.Y. 14543.

Books

Bird, Caroline, *Born Female.* New York: David McKay, 1970 (revised edition).

Brewer, M. Weldon, Jr. *Behind the Promises: Equal Employment Opportunity in the Federal Government.* Public Interest Research Group, 1972.

Chafe, William Henry, *The American Woman: Her Changing Social, Economic, and Political Roles, 1920-1970.* New York: Oxford University Press, 1972.

Epstein, Cynthia F. and Goode, William J. *The Other Half: Road to Women's Equality.* Englewood Cliffs, N.J.: Prentice-Hall, 1971.

Ferris, Abbott L. *Indicators of Trends in the Status of American Women.* New York: Russell Sage Foundation, 1971.

Flexner, Eleanor. *A Century of Struggle.* Cambridge, Mass.: Harvard University Press, 1959.

Harris, Louis and Associates, *The 1972 Virginia Slims American Women's Opinion Poll: A Survey of the Attitudes of Women of Their Roles in Politics and the Economy.* New York, 1972.

Irwin, Inez Haynes. *Up Hill with Banners Flying: The Story of the Woman's Party.* Penobscot, Me.: Traversity, 1964.

Kanowitz, Leo. *Sex Roles in Law and Society: Cases and Materials.* Albuquerque: University of New Mexico Press, 1972.

————, .*Women and the Law: The Unfinished Revolution.* Albuquerque: University of New Mexico Press, 1969.

Kraditor, Aileen S. *Ideas of the Woman Suffrage Movement, 1890-1920.* New York: Columbia University Press, 1965.

Kreps, Juanita. *Sex in the Marketplace: American Women at Work.* Baltimore: Johns-Hopkins Press, 1971.

Levitan, Sar A.; Mangum, Garth L.; and Marshall, Ray. *Human Resources and Labor Markets.* New York: Harper & Row, 1972.

Lewis, Helen Matthews. *The Woman Movement and the Negro Movement—Parallel Struggles for Rights.* (Phelps-Stokes Fellowship Papers, No. 19) Charlottesville: University of Virginia, 1949.

Oppenheimer, Valerie Kincade. *The Female Labor Force in the United States.* Berkeley: Institute of International Studies, University of California, 1970.

Stanton, Elizabeth Cady, Anthony, Susan B., and Gage, Matilda Joslyn, *History of Woman Suffrage,* Volume I (New York, Fowler and Wells, 1881).

Tyler, Gus. *A Legislative Campaign for a Federal Minimum Wage (1955).* New York: Holt, 1959.

Periodicals and Reports

Brown, Barbara; Emerson, Thomas I.; Falk, Gail; and Freedman, Ann E. "The Equal Rights Amendment: A Constitutional Basis for Equal Rights for Women." *The Yale Law Journal,* 80:871-985.

Buckley, John E. "Pay Differences between Men and Women in the Same Job." *Modern Labor Review,* 94:36-40.

Chase, Judith. "Inside HEW: Women Protest Sex Discrimination," *Science,* 174:270-4.

Dabagian, Betty O. *Book of Women's Organizations* (available from Ms. Dabagian at Defense Supply Agency, Cameron Station, Alexandria, Va.).

East, Catherine. "What the Government Will Require." Unpublished speech, 1972.

Eastwood, Mary. "Fighting Job Discrimination: Three Federal Approaches." The Law and Women Series, No. 1, December, 1971. Today Publications and News Service, Washington, D.C.

————,. "The Double Standard of Justice: Women's Rights under the Constitution." *Valparaiso University Law Review,* 5:281.

Federally Employed Women. *FEW Conference Report: Agency Accountability Survey,* 1972.

Fields, Daisy. "A Case of Non-Feasance." *The Bureaucrat,* 1:226-234.

Freeman, Jo. "The Legal Basis of the Sexual Caste System." *Valparaiso University Law Review,* 5:230-236.

Johnson, Lucille. National Pilot Program of Household Employment, 1970. ERIC (from Government Reports Announcement) Dec. 25, 1971.

Johnston, John D., Jr. and Knapp, Charles L. "Sex Discrimination by Law: A Study in Judicial Perspective." *New York University Law Review,* 46:675-747.

Joint Center for Political Studies. *The Black Community and Revenue Sharing.* January, 1973.

Knudsen, Dean D. "Declining Status of Women: Popular Myths and the Failure of Functionalist Thought." *Social Forces,* 48:183-193.

Koontz, Elizabeth Duncan. "Women at Work: The Women's Bureau Looks to the Future." *Monthly Labor Review,* June, 1970.

Levine, Irving and Herman, Judith. "The Life of White Ethnics." *Dissent,* Winter, 1972.

Lieberman, Jacob A. *Their Sisters' Keepers: The Women's Hours and Wages Movement in the United States, 1890-1925.* Unpublished Ph.D. dissertation, Columbia University, 1971.

Markoff, Helene S. "The Federal Women's Program." *Public Administration Review,* 32:144-151.

Murray, Pauli. "Economic and Educational Inequality Based on Sex: An Overview." *Valparaiso University Law Review,* 5:237-280.

———— and Eastwood, Mary. "Jane Crow and the Law: Sex Discrimination and Title VII." *George Washington Law Review,* 34:232.

National Council of Jewish Women. *Windows on Day Care:* A Report Based on a Survey Conducted by the National Council of Jewish Women on Day Care Needs and Services Under the Supervision of Mary Dublin Keyserling, 1972.

National Education Association, Research Division. *Salaries Paid and Salary-Related Practices in Higher Education,* 1971-72. Research Report 1972-R5.

Pottinger, J. Stanley. "The Drive Toward Equality." *Change Magazine,* October, 1972.

Rawalt, Marguerite. "The 'Equal Rights for Men and Women Amendment' is Needed." *Women Lawyers Journal,* 59:4-10.

Sandler, Bernice and Steinbach, Sheldon Elliott. "HEW Contract Compliance—Major Concerns of Institutions," Special Report of the American Council on Education. *Sex Discrimination and Contract Compliance,* April 20, 1972.

Sape, George P. and Hart, Thomas J. "Title VII Reconsidered: The Equal Employment Opportunity Act of 1972." *The George Washington Law Review,* 40:824-889.

Seidenberg, Faith A. "The Submissive Majority: Modern Trends in the Law Concerning Women's Rights." *Cornell Law Review,* 55:262.

Simchak, Morag MacLeod. "Equal Pay Act of 1963: Its Implementation and Enforcement." *Journal of the American Association of University Women,* 61:117-190.

————,. "Equal Pay in the United States." *International Labour Review,* 103:541-556.

Smith, Ethel M. *Toward Equal Rights for Men and Women.* Washington, D.C.: National League of Women Voters, 1929.

"Women and the Criminal Law. A Symposium." *The American Criminal Law Review,* 11:291-510.

Wooten, Doris D. "The Issue is Compliance." *Contact,* Fall, 1972.

United States Government Publications*

Citizens Advisory Council on the Status of Women, *Report of the Task Force on Family Law and Policy,* 1968.

——, *Report of the Task Force on Labor Standards,* 1968.

——, *Report of the Task Force on Social Insurance and Taxes,* 1968.

——, *The Equal Rights Amendment and Alimony and Child Support Laws,* 1972.

——, *The Proposed Equal Rights Amendment to the United States Constitution,* 1970.

——, *Women and Their Families in Our Rapidly Changing Society, Report of the Task Force on Health and Welfare,* 1968.

——, *Women in 1971,* 1972.

Civil Service Commission, *Federal Personnel Manual;* Chapter 713, Equal Employment Opportunity.

——, *Expanding Opportunities . . . Women in the Federal Government,* 1970.

——, *Study of Employment of Women in the Federal Government, 1969, 1970, 1971.*

——, *Toward Equal Opportunity in Federal Employment (Executive Order 11478). A Report to the President,* 1969.

Commission on Civil Rights, *Federal Civil Rights Enforcement Effort, A Report,* 1971.

——, *Federal Civil Rights Enforcement Effort: One Year Later.*

——, *Federal Civil Rights Enforcement Effort,* 1973.

U.S. Congress, House, Committee on Education and Labor, *Discrimination Against Women: Hearings before a Special Subcommittee on Education of the Committee on Education and Labor,* 91st Cong., 2d sess, pts 1 and 2.

——, *Equal Pay for Equal Work, Hearings before a select Committee on Labor of the Education and Labor Committee,* 87th Cong, 2d sess., 1962.

——, *Legislative History of the Equal Pay Act of 1963,* 88th Cong., 1st sess., 1963 (Committee Print).

——, *Summary of the Proposed Fair Labor Standards Amendments of 1971* as Reported by the Committee on Education and Labor, Oct. 14, 1971.

——, Committee on Post Office and Civil Service, *United States Government Policy and Supporting Positions,* 90th Cong., 2d sess., 1968 (Committee Print).

——, Senate, Committee on Finance, *Material Related to Child Care Legislation,* 92nd Cong., 1st sess., July 23, 1971. (Committee Print).

——, Committee on the Judiciary. *Equal Rights 1970, Hearings on SJ. Res 61 and SJ. Res 231 before the Senate Committee on the Judiciary,* 91st Cong., 2d sess. *Civil Rights Commission, Report on HR 12652,* (S. Rept. 92-1006), 3.

---

* All published government material is GPO, Washington, D.C.

————, Committee on Labor and Public Welfare, *Comprehensive Child Development Act of 1971, Hearings before a Subcommittee on Children and Youth,* 92nd Cong., 1st sess.

————, Examination of Private Welfare and Pension Plans, *Hearings before the Subcommittee on Labor of the Committee on Labor and Public Welfare,* 92nd Cong., 2d sess.

————, Headstart and Child Development Legislation, 1972, *Joint Hearings before the Subcommittee on Employment and Subcommittee on Children and Youth,* 92nd Cong., 2d sess.

————, Report on S. 1861 (S. Rept. 92-842).

————, Committee on Post Office and Civil Service. *United States Government Policy and Supporting Positions,* 93rd Cong., 1st sess., 1973. (Committee Print).

Council of Economic Advisers. *Economic Report of the President.* Transmitted to the Congress January 1973. Chapter 4. The Economic Role of Women.

Department of Labor. *58th Annual Report* (Fiscal Year 1970).

————, Employment Standards Administration, Memorandum to all ESA Personnel September 24, 1971.

————, *Minimum Wage and Maximum Hour Standards Under the Fair Labor Standards Act* (Economic Effects Study Submitted to Congress, 1973).

————, Office of Federal Contract Compliance, "Sex Discrimination Guidelines," (Reprint from Federal Register, Vol. 35, No. 111, June 9, 1970).

————, "Affirmative Action Programs," (Revised Order No. 4, reprinted from Federal Register, Vol. 36, No. 234, Dec. 4, 1971).

————, Office of Secretary, Secretary's Order No. 4-72, "Coordination of Department of Labor Activities Affecting Women," Jan. 27, 1972.

————, Women's Bureau, *A Guide to Sources of Data on Women and Women Workers for the United States and for Regions, States, and Local Areas,* 1972.

————, *Laws on Sex Discrimination in Employment,* 1970.

————, "Guidelines on Discrimination Because of Sex," reprinted from Federal Register, Vol. 37, No. 66, April 5, 1972.

————, *1969 Handbook on Women Workers.*

Equal Employment Opportunity Commission, *Annual Reports,* 1967-1972.

————, "Guidelines on Discrimination Because of Sex," Title 29, Labor, Chap. 14, Pt. 1604, amended (as of March 30, 1972).

————, *Legislative History of Titles 7 and 11 of Civil Rights Act of 1964.*

HEW, *Report of the Women's Action Program,* Jan., 1972.

————, Office for Civil Rights, *Higher Education Guidelines, Executive Order 11246,* 1972.

Interdepartmental Committee on the Status of Women, *American Women 1963-68,* Report of the Interdepartmental Committee on the Status of Women, 1968.

President Richard M. Nixon, "Memorandum for the Heads of Executive

Departments and Agencies on Women in Government, April 21, 1971."
President's Advisory Council on Management Improvement, *Women in Government*, 1973.

————, Commission on the Status of Women, *American Women*, Report of the Commission on the Status of Women, 1963.

————, Task Force on Women's Rights and Responsibilities, *A Matter of Simple Justice*, 1970.

This author was also grateful for the regular arrival of the WEAL *Washington Report*, bulletins from the Association of American Colleges Project on the Status and Education of Women, *Women Today*, and the *Spokeswoman*.

Interviews with

Catherine East, Bernice Sandler, Morag Simchak, Carol Kummerfeld, Peter
    Holmes, Doris Wooten, George Sape, Nancy Seifer, Janice Peterson,
    Elizabeth Koontz.

Index

Abzug, Rep. Bella 64, 97, 98, 99
Advisory Committee on the Economic
    Role of Women 82
AFL-CIO 47, 50, 83
Agenda for women's rights issues 81ff
Allan, Virginia 24, 66
Allen, Sen. James B. 52
American Association of University Women 65
American Jewish Committee 68
    National Project on Ethnic America 75
American Jewish Congress 68
American Medical Women's Association 67
American Telephone and Telegraph Co. 78, 81
Anderson, Rep. John B. 57
Anderson, Mary 79
Association of American Women Den-
    tists 67
Association of Women in Architecture 67
Anti-Defamation League 68
Armstrong, Anne 82, 86
Asmuss, Judith 93
Attorney General, (see Justice Department)

Bayh, Sen. Birch 50, 54
Bonafide occupational qualification (under
    Title VII) 40
Bowe, Thelma 78
Brademas, Rep. John 58
Business and Professional Women's Clubs
    16, 66, 81

Carpenter, Liz 66
Celler, Rep. Emanuel 50
Cheatwood, Claudius 78
Child Care
    income-tax deductions 60
    in 93rd Congress 92
    legislation, 92nd Congress 58ff
    mentioned in Economic Report of
        President 83
    Social Security regulations and 92ff
Cimons, Marlene 103
Citizens' Advisory Council on the Status
    of Women 21
Civil Rights Act of 1964, Title VII
    see Equal Employment Opportunity
    Commission
    Court decisions on 40
    passage of 20
Civil Rights Commission 22, 84, 86, 107
    criticizes Federal role in equal employ-
        ment 19, 35
    jurisdiction extended 60
Civil Service Commission, (see Federal

    Women's Program)
Clarenbach, Kathryn 65
Clearinghouse on Women's Issues 17, 66
Commerce Department 89
Common Cause 69
Communications Workers of America 78
Congress (U.S.) and Women's rights issues
    agenda items 89
    investigation asked re laws 90
    92nd and women's rights legislation 47
    strategy for 108
Cook, Sen. Marlow 50
Council of Economic Advisers Economic
    Report of the President 72, 82
Credit discrimination 13, 96
Criminal law and sex discrimination 13ff

Day Care and Child Development Council 59
Divorce, (see Marriage and Divorce)
Dominick, Sen. Peter 52

East, Catherine 40
Eastwood, Mary 31
Economic Status of Women, see also
    Equal employment opportunity
    occupational 7ff, 8
    pay 9
    unemployment 9ff
    welfare mothers 10
Education Amendments of 1972 53ff
Educational status of women 11
Equal Consumer Credit Act 97
Equal employment opportunity, federal
    role in 19ff
Equal Employment Opportunities Act 51ff,
    84
Equal Employment Opportunity Com-
    mission 39ff, 45, 88, 106
    blue-collar cases and 77ff
    Coordinating Council 84
Equal Pay Act of 1963 administration
    of, 20, 25, 43, 87
Equal Rights Amendment
    first introduced 17
    opposition 50, 63
    passage in 92nd Congress 47, 49
    promises legal equality 11
    Ratification Council 66, 102
Erlenborn, Rep. John 51, 54, 57
Ervin, Sen. Sam J. 50, 52
Executive Orders
    11246 33ff
    11375 34
    11478 28

127

About the Author

Irene L. Murphy, a native New Yorker who grew up in Bayville, Long Island, has a special interest in decisionmaking at the national level. She has served as member of the New York State Democratic Committee, as administrative appointee in the Kennedy Administration, and top-level aid in the Muskie campaign for President. She is currently an elected member of the governing body of the Village of Friendship Heights tax district, in Chevy Chase, Maryland, where she now resides. She received the Ph.D. degree from Columbia University in American Politics.